St. Rita
of Cascia

*The Inspiring Journey of Faith, Miracles, and Enduring
Love of the Patron Saint of Impossible Causes*

Written by Saul Cross

St. Rita
of Cascia

The Inspiring Journey of Faith, Miracles, and Enduring Love of the Patron Saint of Impossible Causes

Timeless Wisdom for Your Spiritual Journey

Dear Reader, as a token of our appreciation for your journey into the life of St. Rita of Cascia, we are delighted to offer you two additional spiritual resources for free. These complementary gifts, "The Prayers of the Saints" and "Spiritual Exercises" will provide you with valuable guidance on your path to holiness and deepen your relationship with God. We hope that these timeless treasures will nourish your soul, strengthen your faith, and inspire you to follow in the footsteps of the saints, as you continue to seek God's grace and divine wisdom in your life.

Scan the following QR code to visit our website and obtain the included material:

—————————————— or ——————————————

Visit us at https://motmot.org/93

Contents

Part I: The Life of St. Rita 8

    Chapter I: Early Life 12

    Chapter II: An Unwanted Union 21

    Chapter III: Rita's Life with Paolo 23

    Chapter IV: Death of Her Family 26

    Chapter V: The Quest for Monastic Life 30

    Chapter VI: Life in the Convent 33

    Chapter VII: Rita's Penances 50

    Chapter VIII: Final Years 60

    Chapter IX: Canonization 73

Part II: Novena 78

Part III: Prayers 90

    Prayers for Healing and Comfort 91

    Prayers for Impossible Causes 99

    Prayers for Family and Forgiveness 108

Part IV: Supplementary Resources 116

    Feast Day 117

    Places of Worship 119

    Main Events in the Life of St. Rita 126

Afterword 128

St. Rita

RITA DE CASIA.

n.ᵃ en Sᵃ Mᵃ

Magdalena de M.

Navarro f.ᵗ

Part I: The Life of St. Rita

For centuries, the compassionate and miraculous life of St. Rita of Cascia has touched the hearts and souls of countless individuals, guiding them toward the ultimate truth and love of our Lord Jesus Christ. This devoted servant of the Church, mystic, and patroness of impossible causes has left an indelible mark on the world, inspiring innumerable souls to seek solace, strength, and guidance in her example. With a deep sense of reverence, devotion, and commitment, I have endeavored to chronicle her life and accomplishments, hoping that her story may continue to inspire, uplift, and enlighten others in their spiritual journeys while offering a source of encouragement in their times of need.

As I delved into the historical archives, personal accounts, and various scholarly works, and carefully studied the life of St. Rita, it became apparent that she was a woman of unwavering faith, tenacity, and perseverance. Her journey, filled with numerous challenges and obstacles, never caused her love for Christ and the Church to waver. St. Rita's steadfast dedication to God's divine will led her to accomplish extraordinary feats, transcending the expectations of her time and providing hope, comfort, and solace to those in seemingly impossible situations, as well as encouragement to future generations.

From her earliest years, St. Rita harbored a deep desire to serve God, a yearning that eventually led her to join the Augustinian convent of St. Mary Magdalene in Cascia after the tragic loss of her husband and children. This transformative period in her life marked the beginning of an unwavering commitment to religious service. Through her selfless service, penance, and spiritual wisdom, she became a shining example of humility and devotion, inspiring her fellow sisters and the laity alike, as well as offering comfort, understanding, and solace to those facing similar struggles in their lives.

St. Rita's life was marked by extraordinary events and manifestations of divine grace that stand as testaments to her deep spiritual connection. These miraculous events, such as the inexplicable entry into the convent, the stigmata of the thorn wound on her forehead, and the numerous miracles attributed to her intercession after her death, provide insight into her unwavering commitment to the Church and steadfast faith in the face of adversity.

In this book, I have aimed to provide a comprehensive, thoroughly researched, and detailed account of St. Rita's life, teachings, miracles, and accomplishments, with the hope that her remarkable example may continue to inspire those seeking solace, healing, and a deeper connection with Christ and His Church. As I write these words, I am humbled and honored to have been granted the privilege to share the story of this extraordinary woman who has been canonized as the patroness of impossible causes, abused wives, and widows, and whose life continues to provide hope and strength to countless individuals worldwide.

Organized into four parts, this book offers an in-depth exploration of St. Rita's life, death, and canonization, providing readers with a comprehensive understanding of her remarkable journey. The first part consists of nine chapters, each delving into a different aspect of her story and unique spirituality, shedding light on her unwavering faith, courage, and resilience. These chapters serve as a foundation for a nine-day novena dedicated to St. Rita, presented in Part II, offering readers an opportunity to connect with her personally and spiritually.

Part III contains prayers for the intercession of St. Rita, allowing readers to seek her guidance and help in their own spiritual journeys and experience the transformative power of prayer in their lives. These prayers, carefully selected and compiled, aim to provide comfort, solace, and spiritual support for those facing challenges or seeking to deepen their faith.

Finally, Part IV provides supplementary resources, testimonials, and other materials to enhance readers' understanding of St. Rita's life and legacy. This section includes personal accounts, stories of miraculous events, and additional background information, offering a richer and more complete picture of St. Rita's impact on the lives of countless individuals throughout history and her enduring influence on the faithful today.

Through the pages of this book, readers are invited to connect with St. Rita's profound faith, boundless love, and selfless service, and to be inspired by her example to embrace God's divine will in their own lives. The life and legacy of St. Rita of Cascia serve as a shining light, a beacon of hope, and a guide to all who seek to deepen their relationship with God, find solace in their spiritual journey, and draw strength from her unwavering devotion to Christ and the Church.

Chapter I: Early Life

In the verdant hills of Italy, a pious and humble couple, Antonio Mancini and Amata Ferri, began their life together. Hailing from the villages of Rocca Porena and Fogliano, respectively, Antonio and Amata were not of noble birth or wealth but rich in virtues and deeply devoted to their faith. They lived a simple and modest life, working diligently and offering some of their labor's fruits to those in need. In this way, they embodied the essence of true Christian nobility.

Their home was a sanctuary of peace, love, and harmony, reflecting the union of their hearts and souls in their shared devotion to God. They were a shining example of justice and holiness, walking the path of righteousness with unwavering dedication. And while their offspring could not inherit their noble virtues, God's grace would ensure that their spiritual legacy would flourish in the life of their future child, who would later be known as St. Rita.

Antonio and Amata were well-known and respected among their peers, not for their earthly possessions but for the depth of their love for God and their fellow human beings. They were often called upon to mediate disputes and restore peace within their community, earning them the title of "peacemakers of Jesus Christ." Their spiritual foundation was rooted in their profound reverence for the Passion of the Redeemer, a constant source of inspiration and guidance in their daily lives.

Over the years, Antonio and Amata prayed fervently for the blessing of a child, but their prayers seemed to go unanswered. They remained childless as they advanced in age, and eventually, they began to resign themselves to the possibility that they would not be granted the gift of a child in this lifetime. However, unbeknownst to them, God had a divine plan that would reveal the remarkable fruit of their lifelong faithfulness and righteousness.

As Antonio and Amata continued serving God and their community, their devotion and selflessness grew stronger. They were the living embodiment of St. Augustine's words, a testament to the heart's nobility that reflects God's love. And while their hearts longed for a child to nurture and raise in their faith, they remained steadfast in their pursuit of holiness, knowing that the will of God was greater than any earthly desire.

In the grand design of the Almighty, who delights in His saints and often works miracles through them, an extraordinary event was to take place in the lives of Antonio and Amata. Long past the age when they could naturally expect to have a child, the Lord blessed them with a remarkable conception that would herald the arrival of a future saint. Indeed, the extraordinary circumstances surrounding Rita's conception would foreshadow her special sanctity.

Throughout history, God has shown His power and grace by granting miraculous births to those chosen for great purposes. Isaac was born to elderly and barren parents, while the birth of John the Baptist, the forerunner of Christ and a great prophet, was also the result of divine intervention. Similarly, the Lord intended great things for Rita and arranged for her conception to be a testament to His omnipotence and boundless grace.

Amata was filled with amazement and doubt when she first

became aware of her miraculous pregnancy. Her heart wavered between fear of deception and hoped the miracle was true. She was at times ashamed by the seemingly impossible occurrence at her advanced age and at other times overwhelmed with awe. Amata turned to prayer in her turmoil, seeking guidance from the Father of Light.

As Amata persisted in her humble, fervent prayers, an angel appeared to her, bearing a message of certainty, peace, and joy. This heavenly vision, although comforting, also caused a natural sense of trepidation in Amata, as it often does in humans when confronted with extraordinary or divine occurrences. Yet, the angelic messenger reassured her and revealed the eminent virtues and glory of the daughter she was soon to bear, just as the sanctity of John the Baptist had been foretold to his father, Zachary.

With her faith bolstered by the angelic revelation, Amata did not hesitate to believe in the miraculous birth of her child. She humbly accepted the divine message, and her heart swelled with gratitude and love for the Lord's abundant kindness. This profound encounter with the divine only strengthened Amata's piety and her husband Antonio, as they joyfully awaited the blessed day of Rita's birth, confident in the loving embrace of Divine Providence.

As we continue to recount the birth of Rita, it is essential to understand the turbulent times in which she was born, for it is against this backdrop that God's divine grace and providence can be truly appreciated. Italy, in the late 14th century, was plagued by conflict, corruption, and turmoil. The land was torn apart by warring factions, ruthless rulers, and brutal mercenaries, all of whom contributed to the suffering of the people and the decline of morality, religion, and the Church.

Despite the strife that gripped Italy, the birth of Rita was a beacon of light in these dark times. Her parents, Amata and Antonio, were pious and devoted individuals whose love for God and each other nurtured the spirit of their miraculous child. Upon Rita's birth in the village of Rocca Porena in 1381, her parents were filled with joy and gratitude, as they knew that their daughter was a gift from God and a testament to their unwavering faith.

As the news of Rita's birth spread throughout the community, friends, family, and neighbors rejoiced, recognizing the divine favor bestowed upon Amata and Antonio. Their joy mirrored the thrill experienced by the loved ones of St. John the Baptist, who was also born under miraculous circumstances. It is said that those who delight in the presence of goodness and justice will rejoice at the birth of one destined to live for the common good.

In a dream, God revealed to Amata and Antonio that their daughter should be named Rita, a rare and unusual name that signified virtue and grace. This heavenly guidance echoed the divine intervention in naming other saints, such as Jacob being called Israel by the Lord and the Baptist being named John by an angel. Thus, Rita's name reflected the sanctity that would mark her life and the divine grace that enveloped her from the beginning.

However, despite her predestined sanctity, Rita was still born with the stain of original sin. She needed to be baptized to cleanse her of this blemish and welcome her as an adopted child of God. Four days after her birth, Rita was taken to the collegiate church of St. Mary in Cascia, where she was baptized and cleansed of her inherited sin. From that moment, Rita emerged from the sacramental waters of baptism, adorned with the garment of innocence and enriched with the gifts of the Holy Spirit.

Upon her return to her parents, Rita's newfound purity and divine favor were apparent not only to the eyes of faith but also to the eyes of all who beheld her. In a world besieged by darkness and despair, Rita's birth and baptism were a testament to the enduring power of God's grace and the transformative potential of faith. Despite the many challenges ahead, Rita's life would be guided by the light of divine providence, illuminating a path of virtue, devotion, and sanctity that would resonate through the ages.

As Rita continued to grow in her parents' loving embrace, her extraordinary life was marked by divine signs that manifested themselves in ways that awed and inspired those around her. In one such instance, a miraculous event left all witnesses astounded on the fifth day of her life. A swarm of resplendent white bees, unlike any ever seen before, encircled her cradle, buzzing gently as they took turns entering and leaving her slightly open mouth. It was as if they sought to draw from her lips the very essence of the heavenly sweetness she possessed.

This extraordinary event echoed the awe and wonder experienced by the neighbors of Elizabeth and Zachary, as foretold in the Gospel, upon witnessing the miraculous signs that marked the birth of John the Baptist. Similarly, the heavenly manifestation accompanying Rita's birth was an unmistakable sign of her future sanctity. Those privileged to witness these divine wonders would be inspired to follow Rita's path of virtue and devotion, transforming their lives in the process.

The story of the miraculous white bees has been celebrated by artists and poets throughout the ages, becoming an iconic symbol in the hagiography of St. Rita. In the town of Cascia, where the saint would later reside, a small colony of bees still occupies an ancient wall near the convent gate. These bees, often called St. Rita's bees, have lived in the same location since her time, bearing a testament to her enduring presence and influence.

While not as brilliantly white as the bees visiting Rita's cradle, these bees share extraordinary characteristics with their heavenly counterparts. They are considered a unique species, with a deep red hue on their back and devoid of a stinger. They have persisted for centuries in their dwelling, maintaining a mysterious and awe-inspiring presence.

Though it cannot be definitively ascertained whether these bees are the same ones that visited the infant Rita, their miraculous existence and connection to the saint's life leave no doubt about their divine origin. Their presence serves as a tangible reminder of the transformative power of faith and how God's grace continues to touch and shape the lives of those who walk in Rita's footsteps.

The grace-filled occurrences surrounding Rita's infancy were divine spectacles and harbingers of her future impact on the world. As she matured, her words and actions would embody the sweetness and purity of the heavenly honey that the white bees seemed to draw from her lips. In her life and example, countless souls would find solace, guidance, and inspiration, as they embarked on their journeys of faith and sanctity.

Let us now turn our gaze back to the young Rita. Her parents, Antonio and Amata, were known for their exceptional piety, and it is no surprise that they dedicated themselves to instilling in Rita the teachings of the faith. They were well aware of the heavenly favor bestowed upon their daughter. Yet, they also understood that God's plan required their loving guidance in shaping her character and nurturing her innate virtues.

The vigilance and care with which Rita's parents oversaw her development was unwavering. They sought to ensure that she would remain steadfast on the path towards sanctity, even as she began to grasp the concept of righteousness on her own. As Rita grew, it became apparent that she possessed a remarkable disposition marked by obedience, humility, and innate wisdom far beyond her years.

A distaste for frivolous pursuits and a natural aversion to vanity characterized her childhood. Even in her tender years, Rita found no pleasure in the games and activities typically enjoyed by children, instead focusing her energies on cultivating her spiritual life. Such was her dedication that she would shun even the innocent pastimes of her peers, emulating the example of the young Tobias, who, despite his youth, demonstrated great wisdom and maturity.

Additionally, Rita showed no interest in adorning herself with fine clothes or ornaments, a desire that is often deeply ingrained in the hearts of many, regardless of age or gender. It is not to say that her virtuous mother, Amata, would have encouraged such ostentation; rather, Rita's aversion to material adornments stemmed from her humility and desire to focus on the beauty of her soul. When presented with the opportunity to wear decorative trinkets, Rita would become visibly uncomfortable, often hiding until the offer had passed.

Rita's modesty and spiritual devotion became increasingly apparent to those around her as she grew. Her demeanor was marked by a quiet reverence and respect, inspiring admiration and love from all who encountered her. She avoided the pitfalls of idle chatter and gossip, instead dedicating her time and thoughts to prayer and contemplation.

In these formative years, Rita regarded obedience as the cornerstone of her virtuous life. She viewed her parents' guidance as the will of God, and she adhered to their wishes with unwavering devotion. Her dedication to obedience facilitated her growth in all other virtues; as Blessed Simon of Cascia once observed, "Obedience is the gate of the virtues."

Throughout her childhood, Rita's love for solitude and prayer intensified. Those who sought her company were most likely to find her at home or in the nearby parish church, where she devoted countless hours to meditating and praying. Her dedication to these practices inspired others and bore witness to her growing sanctity.

Even in her youth, Rita embraced the practice of penance, subjecting her body to various mortifications and fasting to deepen her spiritual connection. To make her sacrifices even more meaningful, she would share the food she denied herself with the less fortunate children in her community, demonstrating her inherent compassion and love for her neighbors.

As St. John the Baptist retreated to the desert for prayer, contemplation, and penance, Rita similarly sought solace in her spiritual journey. She admired the lives of anchorites and heroines of solitude who lived in deserts and deep woods, emulating angels more than men. The examples of Blessed Simon, Blessed Ugolino, Blessed John, and other saintly hermits of St. Augustine who lived near Rocca Porena inspired her to seek a life dedicated to Jesus amid the silence and serenity of nature. However, her love for her elderly parents and her obedience to their wishes prevented her from pursuing this path.

With unwavering faith, Rita transformed her home into the sanctuary she longed for. She chose a small, separate room and converted it into a personal oratory, adorning the walls with images of the Passion of Christ. There, she found solace in the company of her Divine Spouse, far from the distractions of the world. In this sacred space, Rita experienced the ineffable consolations of grace, drawing strength from her meditation on Christ's Passion and the knowledge of the world's fallacy.

Although she yearned for the cloistered life, Rita had not yet reached the age to commit to such a path fully. After spending a year in her private oratory, she reluctantly returned to her duties as a loving daughter and community member, likely around eleven. Now feeling the weight of their years, her parents required Rita's assistance in managing their household and affairs. This shift forced her to balance her contemplative nature with acts of mercy and justice while continuing her spiritual practices.

Despite her active life, Rita could not help but feel a sense of envy for the likes of St. John the Baptist, who had embraced a life of solitude in the desert. Though the Holy Spirit had granted her profound insights and divine guidance, she remained unaware of the plans that Providence had in store for her. For now, she was destined to serve as an example to people of all ages and walks of life, living various roles before ultimately achieving her heartfelt desire for a secluded existence.

Chapter II: An Unwanted Union

In the tumultuous period of the late 14th century, Italy was beset by political strife and moral decay. Yet, during this time, Rita shone brightly as a beacon of faith, hope, and devotion. The world was a chaotic and dangerous place, with political, religious, and social turmoil ravaging the Italian peninsula. As the anti-Pope Robert and his successor Pietro di Luna waged war against the legitimate Pope Boniface IX, heresy and corruption spread like a malignant disease. Violence and instability ruled the people's lives, as rival states vied for power and control.

During these uncertain times, the small republic of Cascia was embroiled in conflicts with neighboring states, such as Cerreto and Aquila. By engaging in acts of violence, robbery, and atrocity, the inhabitants of Cascia brought misery and suffering upon themselves and others. Though a brief period of peace was established in 1395, it was short-lived as Cascia soon found itself at war again, this time with Monte Reale.

Amidst the turmoil of her time, young Rita was a shining

light of righteousness and holiness. Appalled by the chaos and violence that engulfed her world, she was convinced of the futility of earthly pursuits and the need to focus on her spiritual journey. During this period, Rita, barely twelve years old, resolved to dedicate herself to a life of religious devotion and enter the convent of St. Mary Magdalen in Cascia, where she would later live and die as a nun of the Order of St. Augustine.

Despite her youth, Rita was determined to pursue the religious life, knowing that her path would not be easy. She bravely confronted the prospect of leaving her beloved parents, Antonio and Amata, who, though pious, were devastated at the thought of losing their only child. Moved by her love for them and sense of duty, Rita yielded to their pleas and postponed her plans to enter the convent, instead agreeing to marry a young nobleman named Paolo Mancini.

The man her parents had chosen was not a gentle or kind soul but one prone to anger and violence, a product of the brutal times in which they lived. Rita, however, was not deterred by his character, for she saw in this union the opportunity to practice virtues such as patience, forgiveness, and self-sacrifice. Although she had hoped to devote herself entirely to God through a life of religious seclusion, Rita accepted her new path with humility and grace, trusting that it was part of God's divine plan for her.

The wedding was a joyous occasion for the families and friends of Rita and her husband, but the young bride's heart remained steadfastly focused on God and the spiritual journey ahead of her. She had already set an example for young women with her unwavering devotion to her faith and her commitment to purity and innocence. As she embarked on her new life as a wife, she would become a model of virtue for all living within the bonds of matrimony.

Chapter III: Rita's Life with Paolo

As we continue to explore the life of Rita, let us remember that the Lord works in mysterious ways and that every path He chooses for us serves a greater purpose. Rita's journey from virginity to matrimony may have seemed like a step down, but it would ultimately lead her to a higher degree of sanctity, just as it had for her role model, St. Monica. Monica's steadfast faith and patient endurance enabled her to guide her husband, Patrizio, towards the Lord and raise their son, St. Augustine, who would become one of the Church's most revered theologians. Similarly, Rita's path through marriage would refine her spirit like gold tested in fire, preparing her for the heavenly glory that awaited her.

The path of tribulation was chosen by the Lord for Rita, and through matrimony, she would endure numerous trials, temptations, and persecutions. He desired her to pass through fire and water—symbolic of the most extreme challenges—to purify her soul and make her worthy of the celestial reward. And so, Rita entered a life of spousal submission, which quickly revealed itself as more akin to slavery under her tyrannical husband. Within days of their marriage, her husband subjected her to unprovoked verbal and physical abuse, driven by his cruel inclinations.

Continuing in the footsteps of her Savior, Rita diligently persevered in her efforts to be a loving and submissive wife and a devoted and vigilant mother. She realized that her suffering had a divine purpose and that through her humble obedience to her husband, she could help lead him to a closer relationship with God. In this way, Rita's gentle spirit, patient endurance, and unwavering faith were a beacon of hope for her husband and children, even as they struggled with their weaknesses and vices.

For Rita, humility, patience, and love were the key to a successful marriage and family life. In an era when women were often considered inferior, Rita's determination to serve her husband and family with grace and dignity was a testament to her deep love for Christ. Through her example, she taught her children the importance of obedience, reverence, and submission to God's will, despite seemingly insurmountable obstacles.

However, Rita faced considerable challenges raising her two sons despite her best efforts. Their inherited temperament and the influence of their father's past behavior made it difficult for her to instill in them the virtues of piety, devotion, and the fear of God. Yet, Rita remained steadfast in her commitment to their spiritual well-being, employing both words and actions to guide their young hearts towards the path of righteousness.

As Rita's sons grew older, they became increasingly resistant to her guidance and teachings, causing her heartache and sorrow. But she never wavered in her faith or determination. She understood that the true test of a saintly life is often found in the face of adversity and hardship. With unwavering faith, she continued to pray fervently, seeking solace in the arms of her beloved Savior and the intercession of her patron saints.

During her personal struggles, Rita remained devoted to her spiritual practices and the disciplines of the Church. She understood that the strength she needed to persevere in her trials could only come from a deep and abiding relationship with Christ, cultivated through prayer, meditation, and the sacraments.

Amid her many trials, Rita found herself grappling with the challenges her temperamental husband posed and her children's wayward inclinations. Despite their resistance to her guidance, she remained steadfast in her faith and unyielding in her commitment to virtue. As St. Augustine reminds us, those who dwell in the heavenly kingdom must endure temptations and tribulations while living among the sinful and the wicked, just as gold is tested and purified in the crucible.

In these difficult times, Rita turned to prayer with renewed fervor, seeking solace and strength from God alone. She meditated ceaselessly on the sufferings of Christ, finding comfort in the sacrament of Holy Communion and drawing inspiration from her devotion to the Blessed Virgin Mary, St. John the Baptist, St. Augustine, and St. Nicholas of Tolentine. While others in similar situations might have sought excuses to abandon their spiritual practices, Rita did not waver in her commitment to penance, fasting, and acts of charity.

Rather than giving in to the world's temptations, Rita embraced a life of austerity, dedicating herself to the needs of her family, neighbors, and the poor. She became a beacon of hope and compassion in her community, tirelessly caring for the sick and assisting those in need. When she ventured outside her home, her modest attire and the radiance of inner peace that shone from her countenance were a testament to her unwavering faith and deep humility.

Rita exemplified grace and kindness in her interactions with others, skillfully steering conversations toward matters of faith and charity. She refrained from complaining about her husband, even when others tried to draw her into such discussions. Instead, she covered his faults with the mantle of charity, providing a powerful example for others to follow.

In every aspect of her life, Rita embodied the virtues of a true disciple of Christ. Like St. Monica, she became a shining example of strength, resilience, and dedication for all married women. Through her unwavering commitment to holiness and her steadfast trust in God's providence, Rita reminds us that even during life's most significant challenges, we, too, can live lives of faith, humility, and self-sacrifice.

Chapter IV: Death of Her Family

Rita found solace and strength through her unwavering faith in God amid her profound sorrow. She understood that her husband's transformation from a violent man to a gentler soul was not only the result of her love, patience, and guidance but also a testament to the power of divine grace working within him. Tragically, her husband's past indiscretions eventually caught up with him, and he was brutally murdered just outside their hometown of Rocca Porena.

Upon learning of her husband's tragic demise, Rita was initially overwhelmed with grief. She wept not for the temporal losses she faced or the daunting prospect of raising her children alone but for the spiritual consequences that her husband's untimely and violent death may have incurred. Her heart ached for the possibility that he had met his end without receiving the sacraments or making amends for his past transgressions.

However, as a woman of deep faith, Rita did not allow herself to be consumed by despair. Instead, she turned her gaze heavenward, trusting God's providence governed all good and evil things. This unwavering faith allowed her to find comfort amid her pain, ultimately leading her to forgive her husband's murderers wholeheartedly. Following the example set by Christ Himself and St. Stephen, she offered fervent prayers for their redemption, demonstrating an extraordinary capacity for love, mercy, and forgiveness.

The tragic loss of Paolo Mancini left her responsible for raising their two sons, Giangiacomo Antonio and Paolo Maria, in an environment filled with ongoing feuds and the looming shadow of vengeance. St. Rita sought to instill in her children the values of forgiveness and reconciliation, hoping they would not follow in their father's footsteps and be consumed by the cycle of violence.

As the months passed, Antonio and Paolo became increasingly aware of their father's murder and the expectation that they, as his sons, should seek retribution. Understanding the dangers her sons faced and the moral implications of seeking vengeance, Rita turned to prayer. She fervently prayed for her sons' hearts to be softened and for them to embrace the path of forgiveness rather than violence. Rita's deep faith and devotion would soon be put to the test.

Over time, the power of Rita's prayers and her unwavering commitment to her faith began to impact her sons profoundly. They gradually renounced their plans for revenge, embracing their mother's teachings of forgiveness and reconciliation. However, the transformation of their hearts was not to be the end of their story.

Before Giangiacomo Antonio and Paolo Maria could fully live out their newfound convictions, they were struck by a deadly illness, believed to be either dysentery or tuberculosis, which was rampant during that period. As their health rapidly deteriorated, Rita continued to pray for her sons, entrusting them to God's mercy and love.

Both sons passed away within a year of their father's murder, leaving Rita to face the immense grief of losing her entire immediate family. Despite the pain and sorrow she experienced, Rita saw the deaths of her sons as part of God's divine plan to end the cycle of violence that had plagued her family for generations.

It is uncertain how long this period of her life as a widow lasted, but it is clear that she relied on God and devoted herself to prayer and self-sacrifice. Heeding St. Paul's advice to widows, she lived a life marked by prayer, self-denial, and compassion for others.

Rita's discipline was unwavering; she fasted often, and what little she saved from her meals was given to the poor. Her heart swelled with love for God and her neighbors, and she found solace in performing acts of mercy. In one notable instance, she encountered a shivering, impoverished man and immediately gave him one of her garments, rejoicing in the opportunity to help one of God's less fortunate children. Her attire was modest and plain, made of coarse, dark blue serge and sackcloth, signifying her commitment to a life of penance.

Seeking solitude and reflection, Rita once more longed to enclose herself within a religious cloister. One day, while attending Mass at the church of the Augustinian nuns in Cascia, she felt the words of Jesus Christ resonate within her: "I am the Way, the Truth, and the Life." This divine message invigorated her desire to embrace the conventual life, a desire that was further fueled by the examples of contemporary female saints such as St. Bridget of Sweden, Blessed Angela of Foligno, St. Margaret of Monferrato, and St. Frances of Rome. These women were beacons of virtue, embodying the states of virginity, married life, and widowhood.

With renewed conviction, Rita approached the Augustinian nuns of St. Mary Magdalen convent in Cascia, known for their strict observance of St. Augustine's rule. At their feet, she humbly expressed her desire to serve God within their walls and don the penitential garb they wore. Despite her heartfelt plea, the nuns refused her request, as it was against their custom to admit a widow into a convent reserved for virgins. Undeterred, Rita returned twice more, each time with greater humility and unwavering faith in

God. Although her persistence was met with rejection, she continued to exemplify humility, patience, and trust in the divine plan.

Chapter V: The Quest for Monastic Life

In this age of tumult and strife, Rita's heart remained steadfastly anchored in heaven, her earnest desire for a cloistered life driven by the yearning to secure her eternal salvation. Amidst the world's chaos, rampant violence, religious conflict, and moral degradation plaguing society, Rita's soul remained a beacon of purity and unwavering faith. The 15th century was a dark time, where worldly ambitions and corruption had swallowed the hearts of many, leaving only a few sanctuaries of righteousness, such as the cloisters, where the faithful could find solace.

Despite her discouragement and rejection, Rita remained resolute in entering the monastic life. Like a flower in a field of thorns, she persevered in her quest for a life devoted to God, knowing that only in such an environment could she remain safe from the worldly temptations and dangers that threatened her virtue. Her aspirations were thwarted repeatedly, yet she remained undeterred, her faith in the Lord unwavering.

Turning to her beloved patrons, St. John the Baptist, St. Augustine, and St. Nicholas, Rita sought their intercession in her seemingly impossible endeavor. Her fervent prayers, fueled by the love that preceded them, eventually bore fruit, as divine intervention would lead her to the path she so desperately yearned for.

One fateful night, as Rita prayed fervently, she experienced a vision of her heavenly protectors urging her to seize the opportunity she had been waiting for: Entrance into the convent that had repeatedly denied her. Emboldened by this divine encouragement, Rita obediently followed the guidance of St. John the Baptist, who appeared to her and beckoned her to accompany him.

Together with St. Augustine and St. Nicholas, the holy quartet embarked on a perilous journey, scaling the steep and treacherous cliffs of Rocca Porena. This path seemed impossible to most. Yet, with the aid of divine grace and the support of her celestial companions, Rita triumphed over the challenging terrain, her courage and determination fueled by her love for God. This arduous ascent served as a metaphor for the spiritual heights Rita would attain in her monastic life, and the dangerous descent on the other side of the mountain symbolized the risk of falling from grace.

As Rita found herself enveloped within the sacred enclosure she had so passionately yearned for, the divine presence that had escorted her there vanished, leaving her alone in the darkness of the night. Her heart swelled with awe and uncertainty as she attempted to process the miraculous events. When the nuns awoke at the break of dawn to offer their prayers and praises to the Lord, they were astounded to find the humble widow, whom they had repeatedly turned away, trembling within the confines of their convent.

Inquisitive and bewildered, they pressed Rita for answers. With humility and grace, she recounted the extraordinary events of the previous night, detailing the divine intervention that had brought her to their doorstep. Pleading for acceptance one final time, the nuns found themselves unable to deny her entry, as they stood in the presence of an undeniable miracle. United in agreement and rejoicing, they welcomed Rita into their fold, adorning her with their penitential habit and formally initiating her into their order. The nuns' delight was palpable, and Rita's joy knew no bounds. As she reflected upon the unfathomable kindness of the Lord, her heart swelled with gratitude, yet she felt at a loss for words to properly express her thankfulness to Divine Providence.

This miraculous induction into the convent occurred around 1413, when Rita was nearly thirty-two years old. This was a significant time for the Augustinian Order, as they welcomed Rita into their midst and Alexander Oliva, who would later be known as the Blessed.

Now, with the omnipotent grace of God guiding her within the sanctity of the convent, Rita no longer needed to long for the secluded life she had once desired. The solitudes of Tagaste, the silence of Valmanente, and the groves of her native land paled in comparison to the divine journey upon which she had embarked under the watchful eye of the Lord.

The divine providence that led Rita into the convent granted her the perfect environment to grow closer to God and devote herself to a life of prayer, penance, and service. The beauty and tranquility she had sought in the faraway lands were now present within the sacred walls of the monastery, allowing her to focus solely on deepening her relationship with the Lord and emulating the virtues of her three holy patrons, the blessed hermits of Cascia.

Rita's journey to holiness required little change in her way of life, as her heart had always been inclined toward the things of heaven. Jesus Christ teaches us that one way to achieve perfection is through renunciation of earthly possessions, and Rita, always detached from worldly things, eagerly embraced this teaching. She distributed her modest fortune among the poor, solidifying her commitment to sanctity.

Living in the convent without property, family, or worldly attachments, Rita found true freedom in her humble service to the King of Peace. She considered herself to be more blessed, prosperous, and happier than those who lived in the lavish dwellings of sinners, surrounded by the fleeting allure of material wealth and earthly glory. Her heart swelled with gratitude and joy for the opportunity to dwell within God's divine embrace, in the monastery's serenity, where she could nurture her soul and grow closer to her heavenly Father.

Chapter VI: Life in the Convent

No one can convey more effectively than her fellow sisters in religion how Rita lived during her novitiate year. They were both astonished and humbled by what they witnessed in her, considering her a model of the purest and most tested virtue from the beginning. Poverty, chastity, and obedience held no fear for her; she was well-acquainted with poverty from her time in Rocca Porena, had crucified her body with Christ in God, and had lived in subjugation not only to her prudent parents but also to a cruel husband. Likewise, the other virtues she practiced during her novitiate had become familiar to her in the world, apart from some prescribed physical penances and the increased opportunities for prayer that her new life afforded her.

Little else is known about Rita's life from the limited records of those times. Still, we know that as her novitiate progressed, she continued her holy practices of extraordinary piety and austere penance. She prepared herself to bind more closely to her God on the day of her new regeneration. Eminent scholars, such as Cardinal Seripando, refer to the day of the formal profession of monastic vows as the day of new regeneration, for through the sacrifice of one's will, bodily pleasures, and possessions, total remission of all punishment due to sin may be earned.

Finally, the long-awaited day arrived. Having first undertaken a rigorous examination of her entire life and identified any blemishes on her pure conscience, the devout novice sought to cleanse them with the fire of her remorse the blood of Jesus Christ. With her heart full of conviction, Rita presented herself before the altar to pledge her perpetual commitment to the evangelical counsels. She did not hesitate to place her hand on the holy Rule of St. Augustine, for her heroic trust in divine assistance bolstered her courage. Although the Rule might seem severe to those entrenched in worldly matters, the saints perceive it as a law of love and a bond uniting souls to God.

Thus, Rita chose this sweet servitude over all earthly kingdoms, considering herself the most fortunate of women as she had finally reached the goal that she had been drawn towards by heaven's gentle guidance since her earliest years.

The exact date of Rita's profession remains uncertain, but it most likely occurred during the tenure of Fr. Pietro di Vena Tolosano as General of the Order. He succeeded Fr. Saracini, a native of Rocca Porena who later became the Bishop of Macerata. This places the date of Rita's profession around 1414. Although historical accounts do not provide explicit details about Rita's emotions on that significant day, one can infer from her past experiences that it was a day filled with love and gratitude to God.

One notable incident during the day of Rita's profession is worth mentioning. As Rita knelt in prayer before the crucifix, expressing her unending praise and thanks to the Lord, she was immersed in profound ecstasy. In this transcendent state, she experienced a vision similar to Jacob's dream in the Old Testament: a ladder extending from earth to heaven, with angels ascending and descending its rungs. At the pinnacle of this celestial ladder stood the Lord Himself, beckoning Rita to ascend.

This mystical ladder may symbolize the ascent of charity, which St. Augustine suggests is prepared by God Himself. This divine staircase enables chosen souls to climb toward the heights of spiritual enlightenment and union with the Lord. At the journey's end, God eagerly awaits to welcome and usher these devoted souls into the eternal splendor of heaven.

No one could understand the profound meaning of this mystical experience better than Rita herself. She was infused with divine wisdom and guidance upon awakening from ecstasy. This heavenly instruction reinvigorated her commitment to seek God with even greater fervor and dedication amidst the challenges and uncertainties of our mortal existence.

The Blessed Virgin Mary, elevated above all heavenly choirs, and St. John the Baptist, hailed as the greatest of the saints even before his witness at the Jordan, exemplify lives dedicated to the continuous exercise of charity. In this context, we can discern the true essence of Rita's greatness.

If Rita possessed charity, then she held all that was truly valuable, for the fullness of the law is indeed charity. Should she have embodied charity to an eminent degree, she would rightfully be considered a great saint, as perfect charity equates to perfect justice. This sublime principle, as proposed by St. Augustine, a master of charity and evangelical perfection himself, forms the foundation of his golden Rule. This Rule, adopted by numerous religious Orders and adhered to by Rita down to the last letter, is a summary of the entire Christian religion and evidence of the Rule's excellence and adaptability across the ages, as Blessed Alphonsus of Oroza affirms.

This heavenly instruction reinvigorated her commitment to seek God with even greater fervor and dedication amidst the challenges and uncertainties of our mortal existence.

Rita devoted herself wholeheartedly to pursuing charity before and more resolutely after her profession. The first indication that one possesses this virtue is the adherence to God's will by observing His holy law, as Jesus Christ taught us: "He that hath My commandments, and keepeth them: he it is that loveth Me. And He that loveth Me shall be loved of My Father, and I will love him and manifest

Myself to him."

The many accounts of Rita's life and the evidence of tradition assure us that she observed with utmost precision all the commandments of God, the precepts of the Church, and the directives of her superiors. Her obedience was marked by cheerfulness and joy as she readily and precisely sought to anticipate commands and exceed their fulfillment. This meticulous observance extended not only to what was commanded but also to the evangelical counsels. Yet, the weight of this burden seemed light to her, as she willingly undertook numerous works of supererogation to channel her fervent piety.

Rita was consistently the first to rise from her bed at midnight, the first at prayer, in the choir, at instruction, at penitential observances, and the works of mercy and obedience. She excelled in all the community duties, particularly when the task at hand was humble. Amidst her unceasing activities and vigils, her sole focus was to find the most secure means of supporting the holy will of God. This devotion produced in her a holy fear, born out of love, that made her constantly wary of even the slightest offense against her most loving God. Such was her dread of sin that the mere mention of it struck horror in her heart.

To eliminate any possible risk of sin, Rita imposed a rigorous rule of silence, recognizing the wisdom of St. James the Apostle's words: "If any man offends not in word, the same is a perfect man." To adhere to this principle more easily, she secluded herself in her cell, alone with her suffering Spouse, Jesus, like a "dove in the clefts of the rock, in the hollow places of the wall." She only ventured outside her cell to seek her sovereign good in the Blessed Sacrament, among the poor and sick, or to engage in other charitable works permitted by her state. Even in these situations, she carefully weighed every word she uttered, and it is said that she would keep a pebble in her mouth to remind her to maintain the silence she cherished.

Rita sometimes needed to speak, whether out of politeness, practicality, or necessity. In these instances, her words harmonized with the emotions of her heart, reflecting her deeply spiritual nature. As a person wholly devoted to charity, Rita's conversations naturally sought to glorify God and promote the salvation of her fellow human beings.

Rita possessed eloquence and fluency that sprang from her heart, enabling her to touch the hearts of others. This is a quality often found in saints that inspires sanctity, nurtures love, and draws souls closer to God. Whether this gift of honeyed eloquence was bestowed upon her from the moment the miraculous bees appeared over her cradle or whether it was acquired through her unwavering practice of charity toward her neighbors, only God, the giver of such gifts, truly knows.

We know that Rita utilized this divine gift to its fullest potential. She offered guidance to those in doubt, comforted the fearful, consoled the grieving, and helped those who had gone astray find their way back to salvation. Through these and other acts of mercy, Rita achieved great success, which the Giver of every good gift graciously granted.

During her remarkable acts of charity, we find it documented that Rita, upon learning of two individuals in the town living in a state of sin and causing great public scandal, wept for their transgressions. She then took the challenging task of separating them and guiding them toward repentance. Rita had witnessed the divine goodness too often not to have faith in her current endeavor's success.

Initially, she turned to prayer and penance, offering them in union with the sufferings of Jesus Christ for the sinners' conversion. Subsequently, she met with each of the scandal causers individually, using her gentle and persuasive demeanor to help them recognize their lamentable state. Much to her delight, she saw them shed tears of remorse and later perform steadfast penance for their wrongdoings.

Indeed, the spiritual afflictions of sinners like these two stirred Rita's deepest compassion. However, her empathy extended to those suffering from physical ailments, and her ardent charity quickly came to their aid. Whenever someone in the convent fell ill, Rita would tend to them, often for days and nights. She saw Jesus Christ Himself in the sick and enjoyed being by their bedside. Drawing from her religious beliefs and the inspiration of Christ's Passion, she consoled them and sought to alleviate their pain.

With great humility, she provided even the most menial and repulsive services to the ill. For this noble work of charity, she willingly set aside her usual devotional practices, unafraid to leave God for God's work. In essence, she became all things to all people, as St. Paul had experienced, her compassion allowing her to empathize with the sufferings of others. Consequently, all who passed away in the convent during her forty years there were fortunate to have her as their caretaker and comforter, taking their last breath in her holy embrace, supported by her tender heart.

Her very charity condemned her to years of complete separation from her beloved sisters in religion, as we shall discuss later. An offensive odor from a sore on her forehead afflicted her, and she feared her presence might be disagreeable to them. Recognizing her exclusion from the community, she harbored no bitterness but lived contentedly in her cell, knowing she was causing no inconvenience to others and remaining in God's grace. She found joy in her humiliation, infirmities, and detachment from earthly connections.

While we have omitted many other examples of Rita's immense charity towards God and her fellow beings, we need only recall her life experiences to understand its magnitude. She lived with a cruel and brutal husband, interceded for his murderers, and dedicated her time to acts and prayers for the betterment of others. Such was her charity: sincere, boundless, benevolent, patient, resilient, and indomitable.

Up to this point, we have focused primarily on Rita's active and practical charity, or at most, her love for her neighbor. Yet, how could we even begin to describe the profound and internal love of God that continually enveloped her heart? The sheer intensity and flame of divine love that constantly consumed her would be impossible to fully capture in words. Her affections reached towards the heavens, God's love transformed her soul, and her inner life embodied the essence of a seraph of charity. To depict this accurately is a daunting task. Nevertheless, we shall endeavor to provide a glimpse, albeit imperfect, into her spiritual journey, particularly when we discuss her profound prayer life.

For now, the reader can form a preliminary understanding

of Rita's deep love for God by examining her unwavering charity towards her neighbors. By considering the details of her life thus far—a life not only free from blame and rich in holiness but also marked by an extraordinary array of divine graces and favors—we can begin to appreciate the remarkable nature of her devotion.

The profound truth that St. Augustine frequently emphasizes in his works—that charity serves as the foundation and life-giving principle for all other virtues—is further reinforced by St. Gregory. He illustrates this concept by likening the virtues to the branches of a tree, all of which stem from the same root—charity. Indeed, Christian prudence, for example, is a continuous eagerness among those who love God to discern good from evil and to choose the most fitting means to please the object of their love and ultimately attain union with Him. On the other hand, justice is a persistent desire in those who love God to offer Him the worship He is due and treat their neighbors fairly. Temperance serves as a restraint employed by those who prioritize divine love over earthly love, enabling them to subject their rebellious appetites to the gentle yoke of heavenly affection. Fortitude is the strength derived from charity that empowers individuals to rise above any hardship or suffering. St. Augustine's teachings on the other virtues align with their distinct natures.

Given the immense charity exhibited by Rita, as we have discussed thus far and will continue to explore further, one can only imagine the degree of perfection she must have achieved in practicing the other virtues. Prudence, the foremost of the moral virtues, was a defining characteristic of Rita and was consistently evident in her exercise of all her other remarkable gifts. It was prudence that guided her in learning the valuable skill of examining and judging rightly, enabling her to adopt the most appropriate means for securing the better part, which, like another Mary, she had irrevocably chosen for herself. Prudence also steered her towards the most reliable methods for regulating her conduct, appetites, and even her acts of penance and devotion. It made her measured in conversation, diligent, circumspect, cautious, adaptable, and gentle-mannered. Ultimately, this virtue, through her long practice of it or, more accurately, due to its divine origin, equipped her to provide the most solid and holy counsel for the benefit of others.

Rita's life also brilliantly showcased the virtue of justice. Her existence was a continuous act of respectful homage to religion, the majesty of God, the greatness of the Blessed Virgin Mary, the merits of the saints, the authority of the Church, and the laws of morality, friendship, gratitude, and truth. Rita was no less extraordinary in her practice of temperance. She overcame her passions and maintained their subjugation to the spirit in a heroic manner through her unyielding fasts and the constant implementation of the most austere penances. It is remarkable to observe how Rita's virtue of temperance, which grew and thrived during rigorous and demanding penitential practices, also nurtured a collection of gentler virtues, such as modesty, purity, compassion, humility, urbanity, and graciousness.

Rita's already extraordinary fortitude only grew in the cloister, aligning with her other virtues and arguably surpassing them as the distinguishing mark of her character. Predictably, the devil sought to tarnish her heart's purity with insidious suggestions, attempting to inspire a love of sensual pleasures and a distaste for perfection. Yet despite his formidable and persistent assaults, our saint, having fortified her mind against temptation from a young age and now an unconquerable heroine in Christ's army, expertly defended herself and fought valiantly. Rather than succumbing, temptation served only to multiply her triumphs and laurels.

It is said that the tempter, realizing his failure in these internal attacks, tried to intimidate her with terrifying apparitions. However, he was unsuccessful, for Rita fearlessly brandished the sign of the Cross, sending him fleeing and demonstrating her disdain for him as a powerless adversary. The flesh also sought to rebel against the spirit, but this holy woman held it in bondage with sackcloth, subduing it through rigorous scourging.

The small world of her convent even tested her virtue, particularly during the years she bore the painful sore on her forehead. However, Rita's fortitude transformed these minor trials into playful caresses. The agony and stench of the sore, the inconveniences of her poverty and mortification, the extensive duration of her final illness, and other similar tribulations through which the Lord tests the souls most pleasing to Him, only served to strengthen and augment her fortitude, kindness, patience, confidence in God, and final perseverance.

Despite possessing such an extraordinary arsenal of remarkable gifts and sublime virtues, Rita maintained the humblest opinion of herself. She saw herself as the lowliest of creatures, ungrateful for the divine gifts bestowed upon her, a wretched sinner, and unworthy of the company of so many sacred virgins of the Lord. She not only expressed these thoughts, but desired others to share her perception of herself. Consequently, she abhorred praise and, when experiencing the profound insights and spiritual fervor that preceded her ecstasies during meditation, she would implore God to work within her soul in such a way that her companions remained unaware, never forming a favorable opinion of her.

Yet it was her very humility that defied her expectations; the more she humbled herself, the more she was exalted, not only in the eyes of God but also of her fellow human beings. And as she continued to descend into the depths of her self-abasement, the edifice of her sanctity soared ever higher.

There is a love that serves as the foundation for every virtue and another love that incites every vice; the former is called charity, while the latter is known as concupiscence. Charity, originating from heaven, pursues three noble objectives—God, ourselves, and our neighbors. In contrast, being entirely earthly, concupiscence has three lowly aims—the allure of worldly success, self-interest, and pleasure. Our sanctification and happiness, or spiritual ruin and misery, depend on which influences are stronger within us. To combat the reign of misguided love and its three hostile passions, there are no weapons more reliable than those that target their foundations: obedience, poverty, and chastity. These were the arms that Rita continued to wield until she received the eternal crown from her Divine Spouse, a testament to her mature and radiant virtues.

The most potent weapon for those striving for perfection

is obedience, and when driven by charity, it paves the way for every noble pursuit. Conversely, disobedience opens the door to every evil, both visible and invisible, in the world. Examining the profound virtue of obedience, which Rita solemnly vowed to practice, it becomes evident that she embodied it to an exceptional degree. All her actions served as acts of obedience, or rather, her entire monastic life represented an unbroken chain of the humblest, sincerest, and most prompt obedience.

Guided by the principles of her enlightened piety, Rita was well aware of the truth proclaimed to Samuel—that the sacrifice of one's will is more pleasing to God than the sacrifice of victims. She continually looked to the example of a God who, for our instruction, chose to live in subjection to His creations. Inspired by the heroic virtue of countless saintly monks and nuns, Rita recognized the immense advantage obedience offered in navigating our way through this world of darkness and sin. As a result, she not only submitted herself to all the laws of the Gospel, the Church, the Rule, and the Constitutions of her Order, but she also obeyed with respect and eagerness all the commands of her various superiors, fulfilling the duties of the numerous roles she assumed. Moreover, she eagerly sought to subject herself to her equals or juniors in the convent, striving to anticipate their commands, heed their counsel, and fulfill their desires, considering herself the unworthy servant of all.

Such a rare virtue deserved to be put to the most rigorous test, as God often examines the virtue of the pious either directly or through the actions of others.

The trial of Rita's obedience presented itself in this manner: The Prioress, having observed her remarkable spirit of submission, instructed her to water a withered tree in the convent garden daily. Rita raised no objections against such an unusual command; she did not argue that such an order was beyond the scope of the Rule's obligations, nor did she suggest it would be a waste of time. Instead, she firmly believed that time spent in obedience was well spent. With her will fully aligned with the instructions she received, Rita dutifully carried out the task for several seasons. In doing so, she emulated the example of the holy Abbot John, whose story in the lives of the Fathers tells of him humbly carrying a pail of water a considerable distance to water a dry tree trunk simply to follow his director's guidance.

Rita's actions were not in vain, for her acts of heroic obedience were so pleasing to God that, as tradition recounts, the tree blossomed again, producing flowers and fruit. It subsequently became known as the "Saint's Tree." However, her primary concern was ensuring that her obedience bore fruit for eternal life, so her love for this beautiful virtue continued to grow. Consequently, she sought the approval, guidance, and restraining influence of another's will in her temporal endeavors and devotional and penitential exercises.

When the opportunity arose to travel to Rome for the indulgences of the Jubilee year or when she faced separation from her religious sisters during the last years of her life, Rita allowed no considerations of fervent piety or personal reluctance to impede her duty to holy obedience. She would not deviate even slightly from this path. Thus, our saint lived the remainder of her life without a will of her own, or, if she had a will, it sought only to do what obedience commanded, ensuring that she did the will of God in all things, which was the sole object of all her desires. This is how she triumphed over and eradicated the powerful human passions of worldly glory and self-interest, replacing them with a generous love of evangelical poverty.

We have previously noted how Rita, even in her early years and amidst the comforts of her father's house, was enamored with holy poverty, observing it through her humble attire, opposition to ostentation, frugality, abstinence, and sacrificing her finest garments for the poor. She even renounced her earthly possessions in favor of the poor upon entering religious life. It seemed there was nothing left for her to do but to take the vow and persevere. Nevertheless, Rita's spirit of poverty intensified during her time in the convent, her chosen dwelling until her death. Everything exuded humility and simplicity there, and she could have been content with the ordinary observance of her vow. Yet, saints are never satisfied unless they surpass the limits of ordinary mortals and attain the heroic heights of virtue.

Although Rita loved uniformity and eschewed the singularities often deserving of suspicion, she felt compelled not to resist God's inspirations or confine herself solely to the community's customs. Subject to obedience, she pushed the boundaries of religious poverty even further. We could recount her prolonged fasts and the meager portions of the simplest food that sustained her, but we will discuss those matters in a later chapter. For now, we will focus on her clothing and modest living quarters.

Rita did not display her poverty by wearing a coarser habit or one differing from her fellow sisters' religion. However, one particular aspect of her life illustrates her spirit of poverty in a unique, even miraculous, manner: like the Hebrews in the desert, from the moment she entered the convent until she reached the promised land of the blessed—a period spanning over forty years—she wore only one habit. This garment served her day and night, even during her illnesses.

As for the poverty of her dwelling, her small room, still preserved today, speaks volumes. It is a modest cell, the smallest of all, tucked away in the corner of the dormitory, with barely any light filtering in from the communal window. The room's only adornments were a few images depicting the mysteries of our Lord's Passion. Her bed was hard and rough, more conducive to discomfort than rest, and other necessities were conspicuously absent. Yet, the holy penitent lived there contentedly, considering herself wealthy and fortunate, particularly when contemplating the nakedness of the Crucified One. She regarded the Cross of Christ, her beloved Spouse, as a mirror in which to see herself.

The divisive words "mine" and "thine" have torn families and kingdoms apart and continue to separate hearts, never passed Rita's lips. She relied on her Superior's will for even the most essential items, always prepared to forgo them at the slightest indication of authority. For Rita, the desire to possess anything was utterly foreign.

On a journey of devotion, which we will discuss later, she traveled with several nuns from her convent. At one point, she cast the money intended for their expenses into a river, or as others say, money she happened upon by chance. Her fellow travelers, believing this act to be imprudent due to their dire need, could not help but reproach her. Yet Rita, full of faith in divine protection, assured them they would lack nothing, and indeed, throughout their journey, they wanted nothing. God, who nourishes the birds of the sky and the fish of the sea, ensured His servant and her companions were provided for during their arduous travels. In this manner, Rita, possessing little materially and humbly in spirit, made great strides toward perfection, accumulating treasures of inestimable value in heaven.

Having overcome the passions for self-interest and worldly glory through poverty and obedience, Rita now faced the third passion: sensual pleasure. This battle would prove even more challenging, as it involved the internal struggle between spiritual aspirations and carnal desires, a conflict that, as St. Augustine noted, presents the most arduous test for Christians striving for perfection. Although Rita had practiced vigilance over her thoughts and senses since her youth, and had maintained her virgin purity, exemplary modesty, and chaste conduct throughout her life, she was not immune to temptation. To triumph over these temptations, she embraced a rigorous lifestyle.

Rita's purity was relentlessly assailed by the devil through impure visions and seductive apparitions. Nevertheless, she vanquished these onslaughts with her unwavering faith and austere penances. During the most intense periods of temptation, she would go so far as to inflict burns on her hand or foot, extinguishing one fire with the pain of another, to remain wholly pure in the eyes of her heavenly Spouse. In her pursuit of chastity, she shunned all opportunities to be seen or to see others, even among her own kin. On the rare occasions when she ventured outside the convent (as the rules of enclosure were less stringent during that time), her presence was marked by such deep contemplation, modesty, and dignity that she inspired awe and commanded universal respect. Rita's exceptional modesty was such that she could often return to the convent without seeing a single individual.

To the worldly, Rita's vigilant custody of her gaze may appear excessive, but as Scripture states, "each one has their own gift from God." Moreover, extraordinary virtues, like Rita's, are not always achieved through ordinary means, and her penances were far from ordinary. There is no doubt that her intense spiritual battles yielded remarkable victories and bore much fruit and that God reserved an exceedingly great reward for her in the bliss of eternity.

Chapter VII: Rita's Penances

Despite its initial daunting appearance, penance is, at its core, a manifestation of love. This love grants one the strength to restrain carnal appetites that relentlessly challenge the primordial, uncreated love, while encouraging reparation and atonement for past transgressions. It is no surprise that Rita, ablaze with the fire of divine love and possessing a profound abhorrence for sin, would push her austerities to the brink of heroism.

Admittedly, her innocence did not warrant such extreme self-discipline. However, in her deep humility, Rita perceived herself as marred by imperfections and shortcomings. She recognized human frailty, the ever-present risk of succumbing to sin, and the relentless temptations of the world, the flesh, and the devil. Consequently, she did not exempt herself from the penances she practiced for the benefit of sinners. Rather, she viewed these acts as a safeguard against peril and a guarantee of triumph over temptation.

As such, Rita's entire life was an ongoing exercise in penance, which she demonstrated through her exceptional self-denial from her early youth, and even more so during her married and widowed life. This was also evident in the fasts she observed in the secular world and the other mortifications we discussed in previous chapters. Most notably, however, was her rigorous and almost unfathomable self-flagellation, a practice she dutifully maintained throughout her years in the convent.

Upon embracing the Rule of St. Augustine, which encourages all to subdue the flesh through fasting as much as health permits, Rita wholeheartedly committed herself to a rigorous and prolonged fasting life. She never succumbed to the exaggerated pretexts that many of the delicate sex might use to excuse themselves from the laws of fasting and abstinence. Rita understood that God is not deceived and that attempting to deceive oneself is nothing short of impious folly. Consequently, she did not hesitate to adhere to the strictest laws of abstinence, undeterred by any ill-founded concern for her health.

Each year, Rita observed three full Lents of fasting and fasting on the eves of all holy days of obligation, feasts of the Blessed Virgin, celebrations of the saints in her Order, and those of her personal advocates. This is in addition to the extraordinary fasts she undertook. Rita consumed food only once a day and refrained from drinking wine. Her meals were frequently seasoned with wormwood, ashes, and tears. For much of the year, she subsisted on bread and water, and as she aged and grew in sanctity, she reduced her food intake to such meager portions that it was considered miraculous how she could sustain life in this manner.

While the prudent Rule of St. Augustine does not demand such extreme measures, Rita's heroic fasts brought even greater glory to the Most High. By emulating the abstinence of St. John the Baptist, St. Nicholas of Tolentine, and her other protectors - all renowned models of penitence - she rendered them the highest honor. Indeed, imitating their virtues is the most authentic way to honor the saints. However, Rita's devotion to asceticism was not limited to fasting. In all other aspects of her austere life, she endeavored to follow the example of her spiritual role models as closely as her circumstances allowed.

The humble dwelling in which Rita concealed herself demonstrated her penitential nature, for it was merely a small cell, austere and dimly lit, resembling more of a prison to which she had been condemned for a grave transgression. It remains uncertain whether there was even a bed within for appearance's sake; however, we can confidently state that when Rita succumbed to natural fatigue, she took her brief respite lying on the ground or, at best, on a plank.

Unfailingly, she would rise from that most rigid of resting

places at midnight to impose even greater torment upon herself. At this hour, she would scourge herself with an iron lash, aiming to appease Divine justice on behalf of the souls in purgatory. Though still part of the communion of saints and recipients of our prayers, these souls endure immense sorrow, deprived of the Beatific Vision and tormented by the flames' pain.

Rita's profound charity evoked the holiest compassion for these unfortunate souls, and this charity strengthened her arm to continue these self-inflicted chastisements. Nevertheless, if she ever experienced compassion for herself, that same charity might have encouraged her to set aside her bloodstained iron whip.

Twice more each day, she subjected herself to the discipline, once for the benefactors of her convent and Order, wielding leather thongs, and again for the conversion of sinners, using a whip of twisted and knotted cords. Despite all these practices, Rita remained unsatisfied unless her rebellious enemy, her flesh, experienced constant pain. Consequently, she always donned a cilice made of coarse bristles against her skin, and on the inside of her habit, she fastened thorns that pricked her painfully with every movement.

Amidst these thorns and the agonizing practices of her life, our saint remained concealed, like the mystical lily from the sacred Canticles, impervious to earthly passions, protected on all sides, and growing increasingly radiant and beautiful each day, as she became more like her heavenly Spouse adorned with a crown of thorns.

As Rita's body, oppressed by fasting, imprisoned in hair

shirts, and galled by bonds, became livid due to scourging, her spirit experienced a different reality. The more her body was crushed under the weight of penances, the more her soul expanded, the greater its liberty, and the more readily it ascended above earthly matters to delve into the sublime depths of heavenly experiences and savor their ineffable sweetness. If her spirit sighed, it was a far different sigh from that of the body; it was the sigh of the dove—a sigh of peace and love foretold by the Holy Spirit the Consoler through the Psalmist to all souls devoted to penance and prayer: "Rise ye after ye have sitten, you that eat the bread of sorrow."

St. Augustine similarly experienced these wondrous effects of grace, and in his exposition of that verse of the Psalms, he could not refrain from exclaiming, "How sweet are the sighs and the tears of prayer! No pleasure of the theatres or of the world can equal the joy of such tears." However, we must not conclude that this interior joy was the primary motive driving our saint to love prayer; she loved the God of consolations far more than the consolations of God. Nonetheless, it was an innocent attraction to her God-loving heart, and she could not cease such dear exercises without feeling pain.

We have already related that Rita received the gift of prayer from her childhood, which she developed strikingly during her early youth. We have discussed her complete dedication to prayer during the year of her miraculous retreat in her father's house and her continued progress in devotional practices, particularly when freed from the ties and cares of matrimony. However, when comparing these accomplishments to her advancement after embracing conventual life, they seem merely the beginning of her purity. As a nun, Rita prayed in the darkness of the night, in the early morning, and throughout the day—prayer, in essence, was her life, as she could not withdraw from the presence of her uncreated Love even for a moment. The hours between midnight and daybreak were her most delightful, offering the perfect opportunity to engage in intimate conversation with God, discussing the most important affairs of eternity and expressing the fullness of her love at the feet of the Crucified One.

In the wintertime, regardless of the length of her vigils, Rita always found the time too short, and daylight arrived unexpectedly. It seemed to her, as it once did to St. Anthony the Abbot, that the sun wronged her by appearing too soon; she feared that its rays would scatter the beautiful light of her heavenly exaltations and seraphic thoughts. Rita never lacked subjects for meditation, for the attributes of God and His inexhaustible beneficence were matters she could never tire of contemplating. The mere thought of being in the presence of God's infinite majesty, which fills heaven, earth, and the abysses, sufficed to elevate her above all creation.

One subject, above all others, captivated Rita's mind—the Passion of Jesus Christ. It almost seems as if she had inherited this devotion from her parents, and upon it, she laid the cornerstone of her sanctity. From childhood, she directed her thoughts, affections, sighs, and tears toward the Passion. The reader may recall how she secluded herself in a small room at home at a tender age, meditating on the sorrowful mysteries depicted in the pictures on the walls and, even more profoundly, engraved upon her heart.

To better assist her soul in its pursuit of holiness, Rita procured and kept certain representations of the Passion of her beloved Jesus in her convent cell.

To this end, she arranged two distinct areas within her cell to evoke the history of the Passion. In one area, she crafted a representation of a mountain, which, whenever she gazed upon it, conjured images of Mount Calvary and the torments Jesus endured there. With deep sighs and tears, she meditated on her Divine Spouse's arrival at the mountain, collapsing under the immense burden of His suffering, His cross, and the sins of humanity. Overwhelmed with tears, she contemplated His disrobing and crucifixion with coarse nails. She meditated with fervent compassion on the brutal blows of the hammer that pierced His hands and feet, and on all the other harrowing torments Jesus suffered out of love for humankind.

In another corner of her cell, she had a representation of the Holy Sepulchre, which prompted reflections on the sacred body of Christ, how it lay entombed for three days, how His spirit descended to console the holy fathers in Abraham's bosom, and finally, how the Redeemer triumphantly rose to new life, victorious and glorious. During these meditations, Rita was always alone, "sitting solitary and holding her peace, raised above herself;" in that profound silence, those tender soliloquies, and intimate communion with God, she transcended passion, nature, and her very being.

Such was her mental elevation during her contemplation of the Divine mysteries that she often experienced rapturous ecstasies to the extent that, on one occasion, her fellow nuns believed she had passed away. Given her ascent to such sublime heights in prayer, it is unsurprising that she possessed, in a singular manner, the gifts of wisdom and intelligence, enabling her to reason about the perfections of God and the most profound mysteries of faith with a keen insight that could not be acquired through study or any natural capacity. In this way, God conceals the secrets of His wisdom from the worldly wise and reveals them to His humble servants, those who appear unlearned in the eyes of the world.

This enraged the infernal enemy of all goodness and sanctity, who sought to frighten the holy nun with horrifying screams and apparitions in an attempt to deter the holy nun from her pious practice. However, Rita remained steadfast in prayer, triumphing over the powers of hell through prayer itself. Through the merit of her prayers, she also gained authority over devils, as evidenced by freeing a woman who had been tormented by diabolical interference for years. Additionally, she obtained the grace of supernatural healing for a young girl who was ill, whose mother was overjoyed to witness her daughter's recovery after bringing her to the saint to request the assistance of her prayers.

It is well-known that God granted whatever Rita asked for, and her reputation for successful intercession and sanctity was so great that devout people, confident in her advocacy, flocked to her in droves. None left disappointed. These were merely the first visible manifestations of the extraordinary power of her prayers. As we delve deeper into her life, and even more so after her death, we will witness numerous miraculous works performed through her intercession, further attesting to the immense merit of our saint's faith and prayers.

Lastly, the fervent prayers Rita often offered before Jesus in the Blessed Sacrament and before the images of the most holy Virgin Mary are worth mentioning. However, it was not the physical location that primarily ignited her devotion. At every moment and in all places, she found Jesus and Mary, along with countless other stimuli, to inspire her passionate piety.

Rita had lived thirty years in the convent, leading a saintly life. She reached her sixty-second year when, in 1443, God chose to mark her merit in a remarkable way by bestowing upon her a privilege that deserves recounting.

During this time, St. James of the Marshes, an apostolic man like St. Vincent Ferrer, St. Laurence Giustiniani, St. Bernardine of Siena, and St. John of Capestrano, served as a bulwark against the depravity of the world, civil discord, schism, and the growth of heresies. After years of missionary work in Bosnia, Hungary, and the East, Pope Eugene IV called him back in 1443 to preach a Crusade in the province of Aquila against the infidel Sultan Amurath II, who had already advanced into the heart of Hungary. On his return, St. James preached the Gospel in the territory and towns of Spoleto, including Cascia.

His sermons in Cascia focused on the Lord's Passion, and Rita attended them. It is not surprising that a nun was present among the laypeople to hear the holy preacher, as the religious enclosure law established by many Councils and Pope Boniface VIII was not strictly enforced until the Council of Trent. Nuns could leave their convents, particularly for religious duties or to hear the word of God.

Rita, along with other nuns from her convent, was present at the sermons, listening with a purity of intention that excluded curiosity and sought only God's glory and the soul's sanctification. The preacher's sanctity, zeal, and mastery in reaching the most hardened hearts profoundly impacted Rita. His subject, the Lord's Passion—the central focus of Rita's meditation and a source of profound love for God—deeply resonated with her. A divine compassion filled her heart, and she held back her tears, later shedding them abundantly as she knelt before the convent's old oratory crucifix.

One day, as she lay prostrate there, overwhelmed by sorrow, Rita fervently prayed to her beloved Jesus, crowned with thorns, to allow her to taste the bitter chalice of His sufferings while still in the flesh. Her prayers were answered: a thorn from the crucifix's crown seemed to detach and strike her left forehead with such force that it nearly penetrated the bone, causing immense pain. Fainting from the agony, Rita believed she could only survive by a miracle. However, love proved stronger than pain, and grace supported her weakened nature.

The wound grew larger, remaining visible on her forehead for fifteen years. Rita found greater joy in this gift because it provided more opportunities to practice humility, patience, solitude, silence, prayer, and love of the God who had granted her such a unique distinction. As long as she bore the mark of Redemption on her forehead, she continuously thanked, praised, and blessed God.

Chapter VIII: Final Years

If Rita's life up until the time she received the wound on her forehead could be described as a hidden life, from that point forward, it became a buried life, invisible to the eyes of others. We shall now pass over an interval of eight years in silence and discuss the events of her life in the year 1450. Although these intervening years were not idle for our holy nun, if she did find repose, it may have been reminiscent of the blessed in heaven and perhaps even more beneficial to the Church than any active efforts she could have undertaken.

The Western Church had recently emerged from a state of melancholy and abasement, thanks to the prayers of the saints. The schism involving the Greeks, Armenians, and Ethiopians had ended ten years earlier, and the glory of that joyous event was attributed primarily to the merits of St. Nicholas of Tolentine, who was canonized at that time by Pope Eugene IV. The other schism, concerning the anti-Popes, also ceased a few months later when Felix V voluntarily abdicated. Rita's penances and prayers surely contributed to the resolution of these tumultuous events.

Nicholas V, who occupied the Chair of Peter, peacefully proclaimed a solemn jubilee for the year 1450 and opened the treasure-house of divine indulgences for the advantage of the faithful. This marked the sixth jubilee celebrated in the new Church of Jesus Christ. With the Church enjoying the recently restored peace and piety beginning to flourish once more, greater crowds than ever before flocked to Rome from all over the world to partake in the extraordinary spiritual favors offered.

Considering the enthusiasm of even the least devout individuals who journeyed to Rome, we can only imagine how fervent Rita's desire must have been to seize such a precious opportunity. Aware that her fellow sisters in religion were preparing to embark on their pilgrimage to Rome, Rita, who had spent years in seclusion up to that moment, was not afraid to leave her cell for such a sacred purpose. Disregarding the inconveniences of travel and her advanced age, she humbly requested the Superior's permission to join the other nuns on their devout pilgrimage.

However, the Prioress deemed it imprudent for Rita to appear in public or undertake a journey due to the offensive nature of the sore on her forehead. She instructed Rita first to seek a cure for her wound, after which she would grant the requested permission. With unwavering faith, Rita turned to fervent prayer, beseeching the Lord, who had inspired her desire for the pilgrimage and had granted her previous petitions. Miraculously, her prayers were answered, and she received the favor she ardently desired. To conceal this divine miracle, Rita used an ointment to disguise her instantaneous healing. However, God's work was too evident, and the Superior had no qualms about granting Rita the permission and blessing she sought.

Embarking on her journey, Rita walked alongside her sisters in religion, undeterred by her age of nearly sixty-nine years or the challenges of the long journey and the season. Filled with joy, she eagerly made her way toward the metropolis of the Catholic world. During this pilgrimage, Rita demonstrated her profound spirit of poverty by casting a small sum of money, intended to provide for their needs, into a river. Though her companions chastised her for this action, God, who had secretly urged her to this act of generosity, ensured that she and her companions were provided for until their return to the convent.

Upon reaching Rome, Rita wasted no time admiring the city's secular monuments. Instead, she focused her body and soul on the objects of her piety— the memories of the holy martyrs, the confessions of the blessed Apostles Peter and Paul, devout visits to the churches, and the attainment of the holy indulgences. One might think that given her stainless life and the severity of her penances, Rita would not need to seek these extraordinary means of atonement for sin. However, true holiness is always deeply humble, and the same humility that led St. Briget and St. Catherine to the second jubilee brought Rita a century later to the sixth.

Enriched with new treasures of grace and eager to escape the din of the streets and the constant crowd of people, Rita and her companions, ever trusting in the arms of Divine Providence, began their journey back to Cascia. After four or five days of walking, they arrived once more at the convent and Rita's beloved cell. Astonishingly, upon her return, the sore on her forehead, which had healed by the power of God before she departed from Cascia, reappeared, making it even more evident that the preceding cure had been miraculous. From that moment until the day of her death, Rita would never again be deprived of a privilege so dear to her.

In the final seven years following her return from Rome, Rita's early experiences remained obscured by the veil of God's deep designs. Little is known about her external life during this time, and only a general understanding of her interior life remains. We can infer her continued dedication to prayer, penance, and growing closer to God.

Upon reaching her seventy-second year of life and fortieth year in religion, the Lord visited Rita with a debilitating illness. This illness would afflict her for four years, culminating in her passing. Remarkably, this is the first mention of any illness in her life, save for the sore on her forehead, suggesting that even after years of rigorous penances, her body remained strong.

One might think that given the multitude of misfortunes, humiliations, and voluntary penances Rita had already endured, she would be exempt from this final suffering. Yet, God wished to refine this beautiful creation of His and elevate her to greater heights of glory by adding to her past sufferings the pain of this long illness. The nature of her malady remains uncertain; however, it is speculated that it was a wasting fever that gradually sapped her vitality, ultimately resulting in her death.

Throughout this period, Rita remained bedridden, inspiring those around her with her serene and resigned countenance and her unwavering desire for further suffering. She continuously thanked Divine Providence for the opportunity to purify herself and merit grace in this life. Despite the many pains she endured, the one that caused her the most anguish was her inability to serve her community, becoming instead a burden on her sisters due to her illness and the disfigurement caused by the sore on her forehead. Nevertheless, her grief could not overshadow her heroic resignation, humility, and patience in the face of God's will.

Another challenge Rita faced was her inability to frequently receive the Eucharist as before, now confined to her meager pallet. However, her holy soul compensated for her physical limitations with fervent desire, adoration, and love, and the internal acts of veneration she could still offer to God. As her illness progressed, so too did her sanctity, and it seemed that she subsisted on the barest of sustenance. The attending nuns marveled at her survival, believing the bread of angels sustained her.

Indeed, Rita's own words seemed to confirm this belief. When the nuns encouraged her to consume more nourishment, she replied, "My soul, fixed to the sacred wounds of Jesus Christ, is fed with other food."

As Rita found herself in this fragile state, nearing the end of her earthly existence, a relative visited her. The visitor spent time consoling Rita and offering her comfort before preparing to depart. Upon leaving, she inquired if Rita desired anything and expressed her willingness to be of service. "Yes," replied Rita, "I ask that you journey to my garden in Rocca Porena, pluck a rose from there, and bring it to me." It was the month of January, a time when the biting chill of winter was most intensely felt, particularly in that valley. Enclosed by looming mountains on all sides, the sun rose late and set early, casting shadows and coldness throughout the land. During this season, nature lay dormant beneath a blanket of snow and ice.

Hearing Rita's peculiar request, the woman was perplexed, attributing her words to the delirium caused by her severe illness. Nonetheless, she sympathized with Rita's suffering and returned to Rocca Porena. Upon arriving home, she ventured into the garden, guided by either curiosity or divine intervention. To her astonishment, she discovered a vibrant, full-blown red rose amidst the frost-covered shrubs. Overwhelmed by wonder, joy, and devotion, she eagerly plucked the miraculous blossom and hastened back to the convent in Cascia to present the extraordinary gift to Rita.

Accepting the rose as a divine offering from her Heavenly Spouse, Rita's heart swelled with sacred joy as she presented the flower to her fellow sisters who had gathered around her. They, too, were struck with awe and astonishment, and together, they joined Rita in extolling the goodness and omnipotence of God.

In yet another extraordinary event, not long after the first, the woman who had brought the miraculous flower to Rita bid her farewell again. She kindly inquired if the saint needed anything else, to which Rita responded, "Since you are so kind, I beg that you will go to the same garden, where you will find two figs, which you will have the charity to bring me." Without any hesitation, the woman hurried to the garden and found the two ripe figs on a leafless tree. She was filled with wonder and joy and brought the figs to the ailing nun.

Upon witnessing this second miracle, Rita and her fellow sisters expressed their gratitude and love to the Lord. Word of these miraculous events spread throughout the community, inspiring awe and reverence for the dying saint, whom they now recognized as beloved by God. Surrounded by flowers and fruit, reminiscent of the bride in the Song of Songs, Rita's love for God intensified, and she longed to be freed from her earthly bonds and be united with her Creator for eternity.

In response to her heartfelt sighs, Jesus, accompanied by the Virgin Mary, appeared to Rita to deliver the joyous news that in three days, she would leave this world and be welcomed into Paradise to receive the reward for her virtues and sufferings. The vision vanished, leaving Rita's heart flooded with joy, which was evident in the angelic serenity of her countenance, maintained even amidst the pains of death. The nuns gathered around her bed, weeping, having come to appreciate the depth of her extraordinary virtues during her final moments.

Through their tears, Rita offered humble apologies to her sisters for any offense she might have caused and imparted her wisdom on peace, obedience, and piety to them. She then asked for her superior's blessing, and her sisters sought her blessing in return as a token of the love they shared. Rita obliged, offering them consolation and focusing her thoughts on eternity.

Although she had been assured of her heavenly reward, Rita did not neglect the spiritual preparations provided by the Church for her final journey. She expressed her desire to receive the Holy Viaticum and Extreme Unction with all her remaining strength. Receiving these sacred sacraments with fervor beyond description, she departed this world, her eyes set on the celestial abode of the blessed.

Rita's precious death occurred during the pontificate of Calixtus III, in the year 1457. She was 76 years old, having spent 44 years in religious life. Her passing occurred on the night of May 22nd, as Saturday—dedicated to the Virgin

Mary, whom she held in great devotion—transitioned into Sunday, the Lord's Day and a symbol of eternal rest. And so, Rita, fortified by her unwavering faith and heroic virtues, entered into the ineffable joy of her eternal reward.

In describing Rita's mortal life, we deemed it appropriate to provide a glimpse of the events and calamities that transpired during her time on Earth. We hope our readers will find it enlightening as we continue to explore her immortal life, particularly as it was revealed through God's divine works to bring glory to His servant. Though Rita's life had become timeless, the world around her continued to change.

The brief peace established at the Council of Florence had once again disappeared from the strife-ridden East. Mahomet II, appointed by God to punish the relapsing schismatics, had toppled the Empire of Constantinople and now threatened the newly-established Empire of Trebizond and other kingdoms. In 1457, the year of Rita's death, the infidel usurper was repelled from Hungary and Belgrade, and defeated by the courageous Scanderbeg in Albania, by Cardinal de Aquileia on the Ægean Sea, and by Uson Cassano near the Persian border. However, these losses only temporarily halted the advance, leaving the hardened and deceitful Greeks with a final, fleeting hope.

Calixtus III, the Pope at the time, was forced to witness the despoiling of Jesus Christ's heritage from his Apostolic throne. He wept for the atrocities he could not prevent. The wise Pontiff made every effort to avert even greater destruction, but European courts' indulgence, selfishness, and rivalry hindered his noble intentions, permitting the conqueror's progress.

In the West, the Church and the world found hope in Emperor Frederick III, known as the Peacemaker, and Pope Calixtus, who longed to see peace firmly established in Italy. The first signs of renewed peace appeared in the troubled peninsula only a year before his papal ascension. Remarkably, a humble Augustinian friar, Fr. Simonetto of Camerino, ultimately brought about the peace that monarchs and princes had failed to restore. Morals and piety began to flourish, providing solace to the Church for its irreparable losses in the East.

In 1457, the same year as Rita's passing, Fr. Gabriel Sforza, Archbishop of Milan and known as the Blessed, entered his heavenly reward. A few months later, Blessed Christina Visconti joined him in the kingdom of heaven. Like Rita, they were both Augustinians. Even the governments of the republics of Siena and Genoa, which had long suffered the ravages of war, eventually found peace. Cascia, governed as a republic, enjoyed the fruits of peace and prosperity, soon to be further renowned by Rita's death and the subsequent proclamation of her everlasting glory.

Scarcely had Rita breathed her last when a series of miraculous events began to unfold, spreading her fame far and wide. The first wonder occurred at her death when a nun who had been her closest companion saw Rita's soul ascend to heaven accompanied by angels, clothed in divine radiance. The second marvel was the spontaneous ringing of the convent bell, accompanied by an extraordinary luminosity emanating from the saint's cell. The sore on her forehead, which had been repulsive during her life, now emitted a heavenly fragrance. That unsightly wound transformed into a shining jewel. Once ravaged by constant mortification, her body now appeared radiant and breathtakingly beautiful. In essence, her soul and body seemed to have been absorbed into the splendor of the saints.

Witnessing these awe-inspiring events, the nuns and the faithful who were present transformed their grief into holy joy, blessing the Lord and seeking Rita's intercession.

The body of Rita was gently carried from her cell to the ancient chapel, where a throng of eager devotees immediately encircled it. They appeared as if they could never be content with merely gazing upon the sacred remains of this holy nun. The final solemn rites were performed, yet her body had to remain visible for an extended period to appease the devout curiosity and veneration of the faithful followers.

Eventually, Rita's body was placed in a coffin crafted from poplar, which was then enclosed within another constructed of walnut wood. This was done so that she, who had been so highly honored by God, would receive a fitting and respectable burial.

Undeniably, the power to perform miracles is solely reserved for the Omnipotent. Yet, the numerous wondrous deeds accomplished at the tombs of the saints suggest that a divine presence permeates these sacred spaces. This holy essence is imparted through an incommunicable virtue, by which not only the saintly remains, but also everything associated with them, contribute to the manifestation of God's miraculous works and the proclamation of these marvels. This very power first accompanied the shadow of St. Peter, as affirmed by the Holy Spirit, and later, according to St. Augustine, was transferred to the illustrious chains that symbolized his courageous confession and guided him towards martyrdom.

Throughout the history of the Church, we find countless examples of similar virtues being ascribed to relics of the saints and objects related to their veneration. The case of Rita is no exception, offering a unique confirmation of this phenomenon. Remaining faithful to our subject, the truth of this assertion with regards to Rita is supported by time-honored accounts, testimonies recorded during her beatification process, and well-documented instances, some of which we recount here.

Before the saint's body was relocated to its new resting place, which occurred prior to 1745, it was a long-standing tradition for the nuns to shroud it with a fresh veil each year. The previous veil would be meticulously divided into small fragments and distributed among the faithful as tokens of their devotion. "Many miracles were wrought through these relics," says Father Rabbi, who cites the following case as an example:

On April 27th, 1652, a full twenty-four years after an office in honor of Rita had been established, a fire erupted in the residence of Giovanni Polidori in Narni. The blaze quickly intensified, reaching a dangerous scale. Chiara, Giovanni's wife, realized that human intervention would not suffice to quell the growing inferno. Recalling that she possessed a small piece of Rita's veil, she urgently dispatched her daughter to the rooftop of a nearby, unscathed house, instructing her to cast the fragment of the veil into the flames.

Fearing that the lightweight relic, wrapped in a piece of paper, would not reach its target, the daughter cleverly fastened it to a chunk of mortar with a thread. Upon releasing it into the fire, the conflagration ceased instantly. Filled with gratitude, Chiara, her family, and their neighbors rushed to St. Augustine's Church to offer their thanks to God and His saint.

There, they encountered the woman who had gifted the piece of the veil to Chiara, a woman of even more profound faith. While Chiara assumed that the relic must have been consumed by the fire, the woman insisted otherwise, arguing that the instrument of the miracle should not have fallen victim to the vanquished flames. She urged them to search for it amongst the ashes.

To their astonishment, Chiara discovered the relic unscathed, its paper wrapping and attached string untouched by the fire. Overwhelmed by this second miracle, the group returned to the church to renew their expressions of gratitude for the divine intervention they had witnessed. The miraculous event spread rapidly, and a public account of the incident was published on May 25th of that year.

In keeping with the pious customs of the nuns, dust, scrapings from the walls, and other remnants from Rita's cell and the initial coffin that held her sacred body until 1745 were distributed to the faithful. These relics were believed to possess miraculous properties, with many experiencing extraordinary results from their use.

One such wonder, as recounted by Father Rivarola, involved a servant of Cardinal Fachinetti, the Bishop of Spoleto. The servant's daughter suffered from blindness in one eye, while her remaining eye was afflicted with a severe disease that left no hope for recovery. Miraculously, the girl regained sight in both eyes solely through the use of the dust from Rita's cell. Her mother applied the dust directly to her daughter's eyes, an act that would have naturally exacerbated her condition, had it not been for the divine intervention of the Almighty. This remarkable occurrence parallels the Gospel, where we read about Jesus healing the blind using clay.

Another individual, Francesco Armilli, experienced a similar grace through the same means. The servant's daughter and Francesco Armilli journeyed to Cascia to bear public witness to these extraordinary events and express their profound gratitude to Rita.

It is well-documented that miraculous cures have been attributed to the oil of the lamp that perpetually burns before the resting place of Rita's sacred remains. Blessed by her intercession, this oil has been a source of profound healing for countless believers.

For instance, Alessandro Alessandrini of Amatrice, who had been gravely injured by a stab wound to his side, experienced immediate relief from his intense pain after applying the oil. Remarkably, he was completely healed without the need for further treatment, and no trace of the wound remained on his body.

Similarly, Granita, the wife of Antonio Vanatelli of Atri, was cured of a large abscess on her side through the power of this miraculous oil. The story of Signor Pompeo Benenati of Cascia, a captain in Ferrara, further illustrates the healing potency of Rita's intercession. Suffering from a life-threatening hemorrhage, he was cured by this extraordinary remedy. As a token of his deep gratitude, Signor Benenati donated a silver lamp to the sepulcher of Rita, the saint of his native town and his divine deliverer.

In another inspiring account, a son of Signora di Giovanni Andrea of Nursia, whose legs, feet, and arms were so severely crippled that he was confined to his bed, found healing through the virtue of Rita's oil. Incredibly, he regained his mobility as if he had never been afflicted by the ailment.

Even Don Sante Mazzuti, a parish priest of Castel San Giorgio near Cascia, found deliverance from the devastating plague that ravaged many parts of Italy during the time of Pope Alexander VII. Through the application of this wondrous oil, Don Mazzuti was cured, further showcasing the miraculous power of Rita's intercession.

Chapter IX: Canonization

A period of one hundred and seventy years had passed since Rita ascended to the kingdom of the blessed, a realm where there is no change of years or things, and from whence she gazed with compassionate eyes upon the ever-changing vicissitudes of this valley of tears. In the interval between Rita's death and her solemn beatification, the world had transformed a hundred times in form and appearance. Convulsions of nature, ruling passions, fallen kingdoms, new governments, shifting dominions, wars ignited and extinguished, ever-changing heresies, ecclesiastical councils, apostolic endeavors, and the barque of Peter remaining steadfast amid the tempests—these were the events that constituted the long history of that time, as they do of every epoch.

However, at the time when the honors of beatification were being prepared for Rita, the world and the Church were enduring only minor afflictions. The overall state of affairs would have been even more serene if not for the contentious succession to the extinct House of Mantua, which led to some hostile movements in Italy, and the discord caused by rebellious Calvinists in France. Nonetheless, those were times of peace, gentleness, and religiosity compared to the past. In the East, the infidel Amurath IV, consumed by debauchery, had lost his appetite for war and conquest. In the West, Emperor Frederick V was keeping heretics in check and paving the way to restore the Church's rights and property that had been usurped. Italy no longer had to endure the roaming bands of armed men who, despite promising assistance, often brought destruction and sorrow in their wake. Moreover, there was no longer the presence of numerous governments, each as ambitious and tyrannical as it was insignificant. Though diminished from its original splendor, Cascia enjoyed peace alongside the rest of the Pontifical dominions.

In this era of tranquility, the arts flourished and regained their former luster. Most importantly, good order—religious and moral—had been reestablished, and the Council of Trent had reintroduced it into the heart of Christianity, where it continued to reign.

At that time, the chair of Peter was occupied by Urban VIII, whose virtue, scholarship, and illustrious endeavors immortalized his name. Prior to ascending the papal throne, he had governed the Church of Spoleto with great edification and resounding success, giving him ample opportunity to inquire into Rita's virtues, miracles, and the ancient, widespread veneration accorded to her. God subsequently ordained that Urban VIII would take upon himself the governance of the Universal Church, and, in the fullness of his power, contribute to the exaltation of our saint. Indeed, the people had already beatified Rita following her death; however, in strict accordance with sacred canons, it is not the people's prerogative to declare anyone saint or blessed. This right belongs solely to the oracle of the Apostolic See. Just as Jesus Christ alone sanctifies the Church triumphant—proclaiming, "I am the Lord who sanctifies them" in the Book of Leviticus—so too does His Vicar on earth, the Roman Pontiff, have the exclusive right to ratify sanctification and announce it to the world.

Never was there a more opportune moment than when the papal throne was occupied by a Pope who had himself witnessed the devotion of the faithful flocking to Rita's tomb and the ever-growing veneration in which she was held. As a result, the Augustinian fathers, the nuns, and the Council of Cascia decided to join forces with Monsignor Fausto Poli and other distinguished individuals, including the preeminent Lady Costanza Barberini, the Pope's sister-in-law, in beseeching him to graciously proceed with the eagerly awaited beatification of Rita. Their petitions moved the Pope, who directed the Sacred Congregation of Rites to begin the process. The Congregation tasked the Bishop of Spoleto with investigating the fame of Rita's sanctity, virtues, and miracles, and instructed him to prepare what is known as the informative process.

On October 16th, 1626, the legal inquiry commenced and was ultimately brought to a successful conclusion. In March of the following year, the results of the Bishop of Spoleto's investigation underwent a rigorous examination by the Sacred Congregation and were approved. The Cardinals of the Congregation presented their canonical account of the inquiry and its outcome to the Pope, who expressed joy over their successful efforts. Consequently, by a Special Brief dated October 2nd, 1627, he granted the entire Augustinian Order and the Diocese of Spoleto permission to recite the Office and celebrate Mass in honor of Blessed Rita. Four months later, by a Brief dated February 4th, 1628, this privilege was extended—at the behest of the Father-General of the Order—to all priests celebrating Mass in any church of the Order or the Diocese of Spoleto on the day of Rita's feast. The Augustinian Order and the people of Spoleto were overjoyed by this supreme and gracious concession, but the solemn beatification was not proclaimed until July 16th, 1628. The religious ceremony took place in the Church of St. Augustine in Rome, attended by twenty-two Cardinals and a multitude of other prelates.

We will not detail the splendid festivities held in honor of the illustrious Blessed Rita, the panegyrics preached, or the poetic compositions celebrating her virtues and miracles. Rita's devout clients competed to cover the expenses of these pious celebrations, with Cardinal Antonio Barberini, the Pope's nephew, standing out for his generosity.

The ecclesiastical pomp was reenacted in all the churches of the Order. Still, the people of Cascia and the nuns of Rita's convent were determined that their observances should surpass all others in magnificence. The joyful pealing of bells that continued for days and nights; bonfires on the hilltops illuminating the surrounding countryside; silk draperies and opulent ornaments adorning the church both inside and out; new paintings depicting Rita's glorious deeds and miracles; the grand procession featuring all the clergy, secular and regular, and every confraternity from the town and region, triumphantly bearing Rita's banner; a group of children dressed as angels accompanying the procession; numerous wax torches and offerings; the vast throng of faithful from near and far; the solemn religious services; the sacred plays and reenactments; and other similar displays all bore public witness to the universal acclaim and joy.

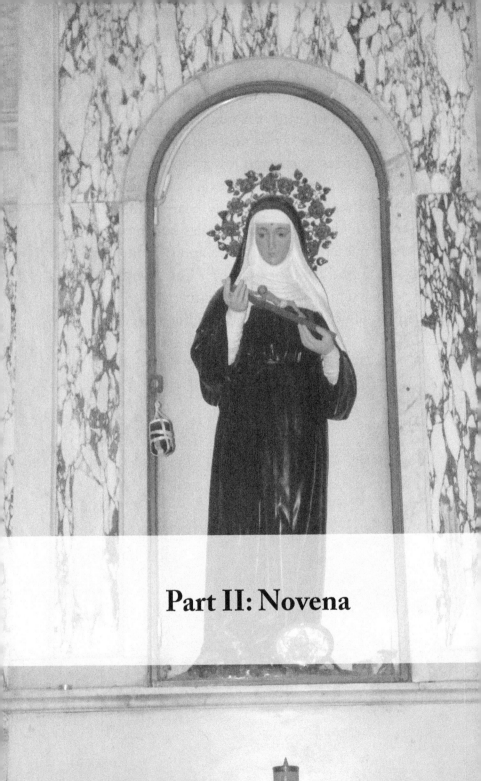

Part II: Novena

The Novena for St. Rita of Cascia is a profound and transformative spiritual practice that brings us closer to God through the inspiring example of this remarkable saint. As we commit ourselves to nine consecutive days of focused prayer and reflection, we open our hearts to the grace of God and the intercession of St. Rita, whose life and virtues continue to guide us on our journey of faith.

What sets this novena apart is its unique opportunity to contemplate different aspects of Rita's life each day. Through her inspiring story, we will gain insights and inspiration to strengthen our faith, grow in love for God and our neighbors, and face our challenges with courage and resilience. We will also ask for St. Rita's intercession, that we may be blessed with her perseverance, compassion, and the ability to forgive and reconcile even in the most difficult circumstances. On each day of this novena, we will reflect upon a segment of Rita's life from the nine first chapters of this book.

As we journey through each day of the novena, let us open our hearts and minds to the lessons we can learn from St. Rita's life. Let us remember her unwavering faith, her deep love for God, and her commitment to peace and reconciliation among families and communities. In doing so, we will draw closer to the Lord and deepen our spiritual lives.

May this novena bring you peace, inspiration, and a renewed sense of purpose as you walk with St. Rita of Cascia and seek her intercession. May her life serve as a powerful example and reminder of the transformative power of faith, love, and forgiveness.

Day 1: Intention for Holiness and Devotion

1. Begin with the Sign of the Cross: In the name of the Father, and of the Son, and of the Holy Spirit. Amen.

2. Recite an opening prayer, invoking the intercession of St. Rita of Cascia: O Glorious St. Rita, beloved servant of God and patron of those who seek holiness and devotion, we humbly ask for your powerful intercession. Guide us on our spiritual journey and inspire us to follow your example of unwavering love for our Lord Jesus Christ.

3. Meditate on St. Rita's miraculous birth and the divine signs that accompanied her life: Spend a few moments in quiet reflection, contemplating the extraordinary circumstances of St. Rita's birth, the deep faith of her parents Antonio and Amata, and the divine signs that marked her early life, such as the miraculous white bees. Consider how her life of holiness and sacrifice began with the guidance and protection of Divine Providence.

4. Pray for the grace to grow in holiness and devotion in your own life: Heavenly Father, we ask you to fill our hearts with a burning desire for holiness and devotion, as exemplified by St. Rita of Cascia. Help us to grow in our love for You and to serve You faithfully in all aspects of our lives. Grant us the courage and determination to persevere in our faith, even when faced with challenges and difficulties. Through the intercession of St. Rita, may we draw closer to You and become beacons of light and love for those around us. We ask this in the name of Jesus Christ, our Lord. Amen.

Day 2: Patience and Forgiveness in Marriage

1. Begin with the Sign of the Cross: In the name of the Father, and of the Son, and of the Holy Spirit. Amen.

2. Recite an opening prayer, invoking the intercession of St. Rita: O Glorious St. Rita, who exemplified patience, forgiveness, and self-sacrifice in your union with Paolo Mancini, we humbly ask for your powerful intercession. Help us to learn from your example of unwavering devotion to God and guide us in our relationships, especially within our families and marriages.

3. Meditate on St. Rita's acceptance of her unwanted union and her dedication to virtue: Spend a few moments in quiet reflection, contemplating St. Rita's willingness to set aside her own desires in order to fulfill her duty to her parents and her new husband. Consider how her commitment to patience, forgiveness, and self-sacrifice transformed her marriage and provided an opportunity for her to practice virtues that would later serve her well in her religious life.

4. Pray for the grace to grow in patience and forgiveness in your own life: Heavenly Father, we ask You to fill our hearts with a spirit of patience, forgiveness, and self-sacrifice, as exemplified by St. Rita. Help us to accept the challenges and difficulties of our relationships and to seek Your guidance in nurturing our families and marriages. Grant us the wisdom to discern Your will in our lives and the courage to follow Your divine plan, even when it leads us down unexpected paths. Through the intercession of St. Rita, may we draw closer to You and become instruments of Your love and mercy for those around us. We ask this in the name of Jesus Christ, Amen.

Day 3: Embracing Trials and Tribulations

1. Begin with the Sign of the Cross: In the name of the Father, and of the Son, and of the Holy Spirit. Amen.

2. Recite an opening prayer, invoking the intercession of St. Rita: O Glorious St. Rita, beacon of hope and compassion, we humbly ask for your powerful intercession. Guide us on our spiritual journey and inspire us to embrace the trials and tribulations we encounter, knowing that through them, we can grow closer to Jesus Christ.

3. Meditate on St. Rita's unwavering devotion to God and her commitment to holiness amidst the challenges of her family life: Spend a few moments in quiet reflection, contemplating St. Rita's deep devotion to God, her constant prayer, and her dedication to her family despite her husband's cruel inclinations and her children's wayward tendencies. Consider how her life of holiness and sacrifice, even in the face of seemingly insurmountable obstacles, led her to become a powerful example for all.

4. Pray for the grace to embrace trials and tribulations in your own life for spiritual growth: Heavenly Father, we ask you to fill our hearts with the courage and determination to persevere through the trials and tribulations we face in our lives. Help us to see these challenges as opportunities to grow in our love for You and to serve You faithfully in all aspects of our lives. Grant us the strength to trust in Your providence and to follow the example of St. Rita, who found solace in prayer and devotion even amidst the most difficult circumstances. Through the intercession of St. Rita, may we draw closer to You and become beacons of light and love for those around us. We ask this in the name of Jesus Christ, our Lord. Amen.

Day 4: Overcoming the Desire for Revenge

1. Begin with the Sign of the Cross: In the name of the Father, and of the Son, and of the Holy Spirit. Amen.

2. Recite an opening prayer, invoking the intercession of St. Rita: O Glorious St. Rita, beloved servant of God and patron of impossible causes, we humbly ask for your powerful intercession. Guide us on our spiritual journey and inspire us to follow your example of unwavering love for our Lord Jesus Christ.

3. Meditate on St. Rita's commitment to teaching forgiveness and compassion in the face of her sons' desire for revenge: Spend a few moments in quiet reflection, contemplating St. Rita's determination to guide her sons toward forgiveness and away from their vengeful desires following their father's tragic death. Consider how her life of unwavering faith and prayer allowed her to find solace in God's divine mercy and trust in His plan for her family.

4. Pray for the grace to overcome desires for revenge and cultivate forgiveness in your own life: Heavenly Father, we ask you to fill our hearts with the spirit of forgiveness and compassion, as exemplified by St. Rita. Help us to let go of grudges and desires for revenge, and instead, seek reconciliation and peace with those who have hurt us. Through the intercession of St. Rita, may we find the strength to forgive as Christ forgave, and to love our enemies as He commanded. We ask this in the name of Jesus Christ, our Lord. Amen.

Day 5: Resilience in the Face of Rejection

1. Begin with the Sign of the Cross: In the name of the Father, and of the Son, and of the Holy Spirit. Amen.

2. Recite an opening prayer, invoking the intercession of St. Rita of Cascia: O Glorious St. Rita, beacon of hope and resilience, we humbly ask for your powerful intercession. As we seek to grow in our faith and devotion, inspire us to follow your example of unwavering love for our Lord Jesus Christ, even in the face of rejection and adversity.

3. Meditate on St. Rita's perseverance in pursuing her calling to the religious life: Spend a few moments in quiet reflection, contemplating St. Rita's steadfast determination to join the Augustinian nuns at the convent of St. Mary Magdalen in Cascia, despite repeated rejections. Consider her unwavering faith in God's plan for her life and her steadfast commitment to a life of penance and self-sacrifice, even as a widow in the world.

4. Pray for the grace to embrace resilience and trust in God's plan, even when faced with challenges and setbacks: Heavenly Father, we ask you to fill our hearts with the same resilience and trust that St. Rita demonstrated in her pursuit of a life dedicated to You. Help us to remain steadfast in our faith, even when faced with challenges, setbacks, and rejections. Grant us the courage to persevere in following Your will for our lives, confident in the knowledge that Your plan is always perfect. Through the intercession of St. Rita, may we draw closer to You and become examples of faith, hope, and love for those around us. We ask this in the name of Jesus Christ, our Lord. Amen.

Day 6: Charity and the Power of Obedience

1. Begin with the Sign of the Cross: In the name of the Father, and of the Son, and of the Holy Spirit. Amen.

2. Recite an opening prayer, invoking the intercession of St. Rita: O Glorious St. Rita, model of charity and obedience, we humbly ask for your powerful intercession. Guide us on our spiritual journey and inspire us to follow your example of unwavering love for our Lord Jesus Christ.

3. Meditate on St. Rita's ascent of charity and her commitment to obedience: Spend a few moments in quiet reflection, contemplating St. Rita's deep devotion to God and her dedication to the virtues of charity and obedience. Remember how she remained steadfast in her novitiate and how she experienced a profound vision of a ladder extending from earth to heaven, symbolizing the ascent of charity.

4. Pray for the grace to grow in charity and obedience in your own life: Heavenly Father, we ask you to fill our hearts with a burning desire for charity and obedience, as exemplified by St. Rita. Help us to grow in our love for You and to serve You faithfully in all aspects of our lives. Grant us the courage and determination to persevere in our faith, even when faced with challenges and difficulties. Through the intercession of St. Rita, may we draw closer to You and become beacons of light and love for those around us. We ask this in the name of Jesus Christ, our Lord. Amen.

Day 7: Courage and Perseverance in Penance

1. Begin with the Sign of the Cross: In the name of the Father, and of the Son, and of the Holy Spirit. Amen.

2. Recite an opening prayer, invoking the intercession of St. Rita of Cascia: O Glorious St. Rita of Cascia, beloved servant of God and patron of those who seek courage and perseverance in penance, we humbly ask for your powerful intercession. Guide us on our spiritual journey and inspire us to follow your example of unwavering love for our Lord Jesus Christ and His Passion.

3. Meditate on St. Rita's extraordinary penances and her courageous perseverance in the face of suffering: Spend a few moments in quiet reflection, contemplating St. Rita's deep devotion to penance and her profound love for the Lord's Passion. Consider how her life of holiness, courage, and sacrifice led her to be a powerful example for all Christians.

4. Pray for the grace to grow in courage and perseverance in penance and devotion to the Lord's Passion in your own life: Heavenly Father, we ask you to fill our hearts with a burning desire for courage and perseverance in penance, as exemplified by St. Rita of Cascia. Help us to grow in our love for You and to serve You faithfully in all aspects of our lives. Grant us the strength to persevere in our faith, even when faced with challenges and difficulties. Through the intercession of St. Rita, may we draw closer to You and become beacons of light and love for those around us. We ask this in the name of Jesus Christ, our Lord. Amen.

Day 8: Trust in Divine Providence

1. Begin with the Sign of the Cross: In the name of the Father, and of the Son, and of the Holy Spirit. Amen.

2. Recite an opening prayer, invoking the intercession of St. Rita of Cascia: O Glorious St. Rita, patroness of those in need and model of unwavering trust in Divine Providence, we humbly ask for your powerful intercession. Guide us on our spiritual journey and inspire us to follow your example of deep faith and reliance on the Lord's plan for our lives.

3. Meditate on St. Rita's trust in Divine Providence and her commitment to accept the Lord's will: Spend a few moments in quiet reflection, contemplating St. Rita's firm trust in Divine Providence, as evidenced by her willingness to accept her long illness, her miraculous healing, and her pilgrimage to Rome. Consider how her life of faith and submission to God's will allowed her to receive divine favors and experience extraordinary miracles.

4. Pray for the grace to grow in trust and acceptance of God's will in your own life: Heavenly Father, we ask you to fill our hearts with a steadfast trust in Your Divine Providence, as exemplified by St. Rita of Cascia. Help us to accept Your will in all aspects of our lives, even when faced with challenges and difficulties. Through the intercession of St. Rita, may we learn to surrender ourselves completely to Your plan and to recognize the blessings and miracles that arise from trusting in Your loving guidance. We ask this in the name of Jesus Christ, our Lord. Amen.

Day 9: Trust in St. Rita's Intercession

1. Begin with the Sign of the Cross: In the name of the Father, and of the Son, and of the Holy Spirit. Amen.

2. Recite an opening prayer, invoking the intercession of St. Rita: O Glorious St. Rita, you who have ascended to the kingdom of the blessed and now gaze upon us with compassionate eyes, we humbly ask for your powerful intercession. Guide us on our spiritual journey and inspire us to trust in God's providence and in your loving assistance in times of need.

3. Meditate on St. Rita's unwavering trust in God's providence and her intercession in times of affliction: Spend a few moments in quiet reflection, contemplating St. Rita's deep trust in God's providence, even in times of adversity, and her continued intercession for the faithful. In Chapter IX of her story, we learn of the 170 years that passed before her solemn beatification, a time marked by numerous changes and challenges. Yet, St. Rita's devotion and intercession remained a source of strength and consolation for many.

4. Pray for the grace to trust in God's providence and St. Rita's intercession in your own life: Heavenly Father, we ask You to fill our hearts with unwavering trust in Your divine providence, as exemplified by St. Rita. Help us to recognize Your loving hand guiding us through the joys and sorrows of life. Grant us the courage and determination to persevere in our faith, even when faced with challenges and difficulties. Through the intercession of St. Rita, may we draw closer to You and become beacons of hope and love for those around us. We ask this in the name of Jesus Christ, our Lord. Amen.

Conclusion

As we conclude this Novena for St. Rita of Cascia, let us reflect on the many lessons we have learned and the spiritual growth we have experienced throughout these nine days of prayer and meditation. St. Rita's life serves as a powerful testament to the transformative power of faith, love, and forgiveness, and her unwavering commitment to God's divine will has inspired us to deepen our own relationship with the Lord.

In these final moments of our novena, let us express our gratitude for St. Rita's intercession and the graces we have received. May her example continue to guide and inspire us as we strive to live our lives according to the teachings of Christ, seeking to emulate her virtues of patience, forgiveness, resilience, and charity.

As we move forward, may we carry the lessons of St. Rita's life in our hearts, allowing her example to strengthen and embolden our faith in times of trial and tribulation. Let us commit to living our lives with purpose, seeking to bring peace and reconciliation to our families, communities, and the world at large.

O Glorious St. Rita, as we conclude this novena, we thank you for your powerful intercession and for the many blessings we have received. May your life and legacy continue to be a source of inspiration and guidance for us, and may we always turn to you in times of need, trusting in your loving assistance and the grace of God.

In the name of the Father, and of the Son, and of the Holy Spirit. Amen.

Part III: Prayers

Prayers for Healing and Comfort

In this chapter, we present five prayers that seek St. Rita's intercession for healing and comfort in various aspects of our lives. These prayers are meant to provide solace, hope, and relief from physical, emotional, and spiritual pain, drawing upon the divine grace that flowed through St. Rita's life and her unwavering commitment to the love and mercy of our Lord Jesus Christ. As you recite these prayers, may you be inspired by St. Rita's resilience, faith, and compassion, and may her intercession bring healing and comfort to you and your loved ones in times of need.

Prayer for Emotional Healing through St. Rita's Intercession

O Loving God, through the intercession of Saint Rita, who bore her sufferings with such grace and fortitude, we humbly beseech You to bestow Your divine healing upon those who are burdened by emotional pain and turmoil. May they, through the example of St. Rita, find solace in Your loving embrace and be granted the grace to endure their trials with patience and courage.

We implore You, O Most Merciful Father, to touch the hearts of the afflicted and break the chains of despair and desolation that bind them. Instill within them a renewed sense of hope and trust in Your infinite wisdom, as they turn to You in their time of need. Through the powerful intercession of St. Rita, may they be granted the strength to persevere, knowing that their emotional anguish will be transformed into an opportunity for spiritual growth and a deepening of their relationship with You.

We ask You, O Lord, to send forth Your Holy Spirit to guide and comfort them in their journey towards healing. May they be enlightened to recognize and accept the love and support of those around them, and to be reminded that they are never alone in their struggles. May the light of Your divine presence, O Heavenly Father, dispel the shadows of fear and doubt that may cloud their minds and hearts, allowing them to experience Your unfailing love and compassion.

Through St. Rita's intercession, we also pray for their families and friends who suffer alongside them, that they may be granted the grace to provide the necessary understanding, encouragement, and support. May they be a beacon of Your love and a reflection of Your tender mercy, as they stand by their loved ones in their time of need.

O Heavenly Father, in Your immeasurable love and mercy, please grant complete emotional healing to those who seek Your help. By the powerful intercession of St. Rita, may they experience the depth of Your love and the warmth of Your embrace, as they are restored to wholeness and peace in Your divine presence. We ask this through Christ our Lord, who lives and reigns with You and the Holy Spirit, one God, forever and ever. Amen.

St. Rita's Prayer for Physical Healing

O glorious St. Rita, patroness of the afflicted and advocate of the hopeless, we come before you seeking your powerful intercession in our time of need. You, who bore your own suffering with unwavering faith and unyielding perseverance, are a testament to the healing power of God's grace. With deep reverence, we implore your aid as we seek physical healing and comfort.

In your earthly life, you encountered trials and tribulations that tested your faith and brought you closer to the divine mercy of our Lord Jesus Christ. You bore the pain of Christ's crown of thorns upon your brow, a visible sign of your union with His suffering. O St. Rita, we trust in your intimate connection with the Divine Physician, and we beseech you to intercede on our behalf for the restoration of health and the alleviation of suffering for those in need of physical healing.

By the wounds of Christ, we ask for your assistance in alleviating the pains and ailments that afflict our bodies, for we know that nothing is impossible for God. May His healing presence be made manifest in our lives, and may our suffering be transformed into a wellspring of grace, drawing us ever closer to the Sacred Heart of Jesus. In His infinite love, may He grant us the strength to endure our trials with patience, hope, and unwavering faith.

Dearest St. Rita, help us to find solace in the midst of our suffering, and to trust that God's plan for our lives is always guided by divine providence. Through your intercession, may we be granted the wisdom to accept the healing God offers us, whether it be of body or spirit. May our hearts remain steadfast in the love of Christ, and may our lives become a testament to the transformative power of His healing grace.

In your compassionate heart, O St. Rita, we place our trust and our hope. With humble confidence, we implore your powerful intercession before the throne of God. Obtain for us the physical healing we seek, and above all, the grace to accept God's will in all things. Through your prayers, may we be granted the serenity and comfort to persevere through our trials, and may our hearts be ever united with the suffering Christ and the hope of eternal salvation. Amen.

Prayer for Healing Relationships with St. Rita

O Most Merciful St. Rita, heavenly patroness of healing and comfort, we come to you in our time of need, seeking solace and intercession as we face the challenges of healing our relationships. In your infinite wisdom and divine grace, you have shown us the power of forgiveness and the beauty of reconciliation through your unwavering faith and devotion to our Lord Jesus Christ. We humbly beseech you to guide us in our journey of healing, as we strive to mend the fractures and misunderstandings that have come between us and our loved ones.

We implore your divine intercession, O St. Rita, to soften our hearts and open our minds, so that we may let go of our grievances and resentments. Instill in us the virtues of patience and understanding, so that we can listen with open hearts and compassionate souls to the needs and concerns of those we hold dear. Help us to recognize and acknowledge our own faults and shortcomings, as we learn to accept the imperfections of others. Grant us the wisdom to discern when to speak and when to remain silent, as we seek to build bridges of communication and understanding.

O St. Rita, who faced the trials and tribulations of a difficult marriage and family life with grace and resilience, guide us as we endeavor to heal and restore the bonds that have been tested and strained by the hardships of this earthly life. Empower us with the strength to persevere through the pain and suffering, and the courage to embrace the transformative power of forgiveness, healing, and redemption in our relationships. Through your intercession, may we become living witnesses to the mercy and love of our Lord Jesus Christ, as we seek to embody His teachings in our daily lives.

We ask you, O St. Rita, to intercede on our behalf and implore our Heavenly Father to bestow upon us His divine grace and blessing. May the Holy Spirit, the Comforter, be our constant companion, guiding and sustaining us on our journey toward healing and reconciliation. Through the precious blood of our Lord Jesus Christ, may we find solace, strength, and renewed hope as we work to mend the fabric of our relationships and restore the bonds of love and trust that unite us as children of God.

In union with the Holy Trinity—Father, Son, and Holy Spirit—we offer our prayers, our hopes, and our hearts to you, O Glorious St. Rita, trusting in your powerful intercession and your unwavering devotion to our Lord and Savior, Jesus Christ. Amen.

St. Rita's Prayer for Comfort in Times of Loss

O Glorious St. Rita, patroness of those who are suffering and in need of consolation, we come before you in our time of loss, seeking your intercession and heavenly aid. Your life on earth was marked by sorrow and pain, yet you always found solace in the loving embrace of our Lord Jesus Christ. May we, too, find comfort in His presence as we face the challenges and grief that life brings.

In the depths of our despair, help us to remember the love and compassion of our Heavenly Father, who sent His only Son to suffer and die for our salvation. May we unite our sufferings with His, and in doing so, find meaning and purpose in our pain. Through your powerful intercession, may we experience the healing touch of the Divine Physician, who alone can mend our broken hearts and fill us with His grace.

St. Rita, you who bore your own losses with patience and trust in God's divine plan, guide us as we navigate the murky waters of sorrow and despair. Instill in us the virtues of faith, hope, and charity that we may face our trials with courage and perseverance. Help us to accept the will of God in our lives, and to find peace in knowing that His plan is always for our good, even in the face of great adversity.

As we mourn the loss of our loved ones, bring to our hearts the consoling words of our Lord Jesus Christ, who promised that He would not leave us orphans, but would send the Holy Spirit to be our Comforter and Advocate. May the presence of the Holy Spirit fill us with strength and fortitude, so that we may continue to walk in faith, even amidst the darkness that surrounds us.

O compassionate St. Rita, in your great wisdom, you understood that suffering and loss are inevitable parts of our earthly pilgrimage. Teach us to embrace our crosses with love, as you did, knowing that in doing so, we are following the footsteps of our Savior. May our hearts be united with His Sacred Heart, and through your intercession, may we find solace and healing in the tender embrace of His infinite mercy.

We ask this through our Lord Jesus Christ, who lives and reigns with the Father and the Holy Spirit, one God, forever and ever. Amen.

Prayer for Inner Peace and Serenity through St. Rita's Guidance

O Heavenly Father, Almighty and Everlasting, we come before You in humble supplication, seeking Your divine guidance and the intercession of St. Rita, the saint of impossible causes and a beacon of hope for those in distress. Through her unwavering devotion and faith, we beseech You to grant us inner peace and serenity in times of turmoil and uncertainty. May our hearts be opened to Your loving presence, and may our spirits be soothed by Your infinite mercy and grace.

In our moments of weakness, when darkness threatens to consume us, we ask St. Rita to be our guiding light, leading us to the path of spiritual healing and comfort. May her life of sacrifice and piety serve as an inspiration for us to overcome the storms of life, always trusting in Your divine providence and the promise of eternal peace. With St. Rita's intercession, we ask You, Lord, to fill our hearts with an unshakeable faith, unwavering hope, and selfless love.

As we traverse this earthly pilgrimage, may the example of St. Rita's perseverance in times of adversity remind us of Your abiding love and presence. In her suffering, she embraced the cross and found solace in Your divine will. We pray that, through her guidance, we too may find the strength to bear our burdens with grace and humility, secure in the knowledge that Your loving hand will guide and protect us in our journey.

In moments of despair, when we struggle to find meaning and purpose, we ask St. Rita to intercede on our behalf, beseeching You to grant us clarity of mind and tranquility of spirit. May we learn to accept Your divine plan for our lives, trusting that, in Your infinite wisdom and love, You will lead us to inner peace and serenity. Through St. Rita's intercession, may we find solace in Your embrace, and may our hearts be filled with an unending desire to serve You faithfully and unreservedly.

We implore You, O Heavenly Father, through the intercession of St. Rita, to grant us the grace to persevere in faith and trust, even in the midst of the most trying circumstances. As we navigate the challenges and tribulations of this world, may we always turn to You for refuge, seeking Your divine guidance and the intercession of St. Rita to bring about the healing and comfort our souls so desperately need. Amen.

Prayers for Impossible Causes

In moments of despair, when all hope seems lost, St. Rita serves as a powerful intercessor, guiding us through our darkest hours and helping us to find solace and strength in our Lord Jesus Christ. By seeking her intercession, we turn to a saint who intimately understands the pain and heartache that life can bring and who has proven time and again her ability to intercede for those in the most desperate of situations.

In this chapter, we present five powerful prayers for impossible causes, seeking the intercession of St. Rita. These prayers serve as a testament to the profound faith and trust we place in her guidance and her ability to bring our petitions before the Lord. As you pray, remember the resilience and unwavering faith that characterized St. Rita's life, and let her example inspire you to face your own challenges with courage and hope.

St. Rita's Intercession for Miracles and Divine Intervention

O Saint Rita, humble servant of the Lord and compassionate advocate for those in need, you who have faced the impossible and witnessed the miraculous in your own life, we approach you in humble supplication. In our darkest hours, when hope fades and despair threatens to engulf us, we turn to you as a beacon of faith, a shining example of resilience and unwavering trust in God's divine providence. We beseech your powerful intercession for miracles and divine intervention, for you have known the depths of sorrow and the heights of joy, and through it all, have remained steadfast in your devotion to our Heavenly Father.

In your wisdom and holiness, you have shown us the power of prayer and the strength that comes from surrendering to the will of God. We now ask you, O Patroness of Impossible Causes, to intercede on our behalf and bring our petitions before the throne of grace. May the Almighty God, who granted you the gift of miracles in your earthly life, hear our prayers and, through your intercession, grant us the miracles we seek in our time of need.

We implore you, O Saint Rita, to stand beside us in our trials and tribulations, to guide us in discerning the divine will, and to strengthen our resolve to persevere in faith, hope, and charity. As we journey through the storms of life, may your compassionate spirit and unwavering devotion inspire us to seek the face of Christ in all we do and to trust in the boundless mercy of God.

In your enduring love for the suffering and afflicted, you have been a source of comfort and solace to countless souls, offering hope and healing to those who have lost their way. We humbly ask you to intercede for us now, that we too may find consolation in the midst of our pain, and that through your prayers, the miraculous grace of God may transform our impossible causes into testimonies of triumph and divine intervention.

With hearts full of gratitude and trust in your intercession, we implore your aid in our hour of need, O Saint Rita, knowing that the God who worked wonders through you in your earthly life continues to do so in the lives of those who earnestly seek His face. We place our hope and confidence in the divine plan of our Heavenly Father, and we beseech you to present our petitions to Him, that by your prayers and merits, we may obtain the miracles we seek and give glory to His holy name.

Saint Rita, model of patience and virtue, beacon of hope in times of despair, pray for us and intercede for our impossible causes. May your prayers lead us to the miracles and divine intervention we seek, that we may witness firsthand the power and love of our merciful God, who is our refuge and our strength, now and forevermore. Amen.

St. Rita's Prayer for Help in Desperate Situations

O glorious St. Rita, beacon of hope and solace in our darkest hours, to whom we turn in times of despair and anguish, we beseech you with humble and contrite hearts to intercede for us in our most challenging moments. You, who have been rightly called the saint of the impossible, have shown us the power of faith, the triumph of love, and the grace of God, even in the face of insurmountable obstacles. Incline your ear to our pleas and present our cause before the throne of the Most High.

In the depths of our suffering, we seek your intercession, for you have known sorrow, heartache, and the wounds of injustice. You have shared in the bitter cup of grief, yet your unwavering faith and unyielding trust in God's divine providence have led you through the darkest valleys of despair to the heights of heavenly peace. Teach us, O holy patroness of the afflicted, to persevere in our tribulations, to trust in the divine will of our Heavenly Father, and to surrender ourselves entirely to His infinite wisdom and mercy.

O compassionate St. Rita, we implore your help in our desperate situation, confident in your boundless love and the miracles wrought through your intercession. As you bore the stigmata of Christ's passion and lovingly embraced the thorns that pierced your brow, may we, too, find solace in uniting our suffering with the Passion of our Lord Jesus Christ. Grant us the courage to bear our crosses with patience, the strength to endure our trials with hope, and the grace to transform our pain into a wellspring of divine love.

Through your powerful intercession, dear St. Rita, may our impossible cause find favor with God, and may His divine intervention bring about the resolution we so ardently desire. But above all, may His will be done in our lives, as we strive to conform ourselves to the image of His Son and seek the salvation of our souls. Help us to trust in the unfathomable depths of His love and mercy, knowing that all things work together for the good of those who love Him and are called according to His purpose.

O St. Rita, we place our trust in your intercession and in the boundless love and mercy of our Lord Jesus Christ. May our prayers be pleasing in His sight, and may we experience the power of His grace in our lives. Through your intercession, may we receive the strength, the wisdom, and the faith we need to face our trials and to overcome the seemingly impossible challenges before us. We ask this with confidence in your powerful patronage and in the name of our Lord Jesus Christ, who lives and reigns with the Father and the Holy Spirit, one God, forever and ever. Amen.

Prayer for St. Rita's Intervention in Hopeless Cases

O most compassionate and glorious St. Rita, advocate of the most hopeless and desperate causes, in this moment of great need, I turn to you with confidence and humility, seeking your powerful intercession. Through the countless miracles you have obtained for those in the most dire straits, I implore your heavenly aid to rescue me from this seemingly insurmountable trial. As a vessel of God's mercy and grace, may your boundless love and unwavering faith shine upon me and envelop me in the warmth of divine consolation.

In the dark hour of my tribulation, when my heart is heavy and my spirit is faint, I beseech you, St. Rita, to be my guiding light and my beacon of hope. Enlighten my path, that I may discern the will of the Lord in the face of overwhelming adversity. Strengthen my resolve, that I may persevere in my faith and trust in God's unfailing love, even when all seems lost. Fortify my heart, that I may endure this ordeal with courage and serenity, and emerge victorious, transformed by the Lord's grace and mercy.

Dear St. Rita, through your own life, you have demonstrated the transformative power of God's love in the most challenging circumstances. You bore your sufferings with unwavering patience and complete surrender to the divine will. I implore you to obtain for me the same spirit of resignation and acceptance, that I may trust in God's plan for me, even when I cannot comprehend its wisdom. Instill in me the faith to believe that the Lord will never abandon me, and that He will guide me through the darkest valleys of my life.

As I face the seemingly insurmountable obstacles before me, O St. Rita, I humbly ask for your heavenly intercession. Implore the Lord to grant me the grace to bear my cross with fortitude, to find solace in His divine presence, and to draw strength from His infinite love. May my heart be filled with the peace that surpasses all understanding, knowing that my prayers are heard and that my deliverance is at hand.

O gracious St. Rita, I thank you for your loving intercession on my behalf, and I promise to remember and honor your unwavering faith and devotion to our Lord Jesus Christ. May your example inspire me to remain steadfast in my faith, to trust in God's providence, and to be a beacon of hope and love to all those who suffer. Through your powerful prayers and the merits of our Redeemer, Jesus Christ, may I emerge from this desperate situation renewed in spirit, grateful for the Lord's infinite mercy, and resolute in my commitment to follow His path for the rest of my days. Amen.

St. Rita's Miracle Prayer for the Impossible

O glorious St. Rita, mighty intercessor in the most desperate and hopeless of circumstances, we come before you today with hearts filled with faith and confidence in your miraculous aid. We beseech you to hear our humble prayer and to present our petitions before the throne of God, that He may grant us the graces we so desperately seek.

In your earthly life, you experienced the depths of suffering and sorrow, and through these trials, you remained unwavering in your faith and steadfast in your love for God.

You became a beacon of hope and perseverance, shining brightly as a testament to the power of God's love and mercy. It is with great trust in your intercession, O miraculous St. Rita, that we implore your assistance in our time of need.

St. Rita's Miracle Prayer for the Impossible

O most compassionate St. Rita, patroness of the impossible, we implore your intercession in our moment of utter desperation. You, who bore the wounds of Christ with such patience and fortitude, understand the depths of our anguish and the weight of the crosses we carry. We humbly ask that you present our cause to the Lord, that He may grant us the miracle we so desperately seek.

As we face the seemingly insurmountable obstacles before us, we remember your own trials and tribulations, which were overcome through your unwavering faith and ardent love for God. We ask that you inspire within us that same spirit of perseverance, that we may face our challenges with courage and confidence, knowing that the Lord is with us and will never abandon us in our hour of need.

Through your miraculous intercession, O St. Rita, may our impossible cause find favor with God, and may His infinite wisdom guide us to the resolution we seek. Help us to bear our crosses with patience and grace, trusting that the Lord's will shall be done, and that His loving plan for us will ultimately prevail.

In our darkest moments, when all seems lost and hopelessness threatens to overwhelm us, remind us, O St. Rita, of the power of prayer and the boundless love of our Heavenly Father. Encourage us to surrender our cares and concerns to His divine providence, knowing that He will provide for all our needs in accordance with His perfect will.

We thank you, O St. Rita, for your unfailing intercession and for the miracles wrought through your prayers. May our lives, like yours, be a testament to the power of faith and the love of God, and may we, through your heavenly assistance, overcome the impossible and emerge victorious in His name.

Amen.

Prayer to St. Rita for the Resolution of Seemingly Insurmountable Problems

O glorious St. Rita, beacon of hope and solace in the face of adversity, we come before you with humble hearts to implore your powerful intercession. You, who bore the weight of life's trials and tribulations with unwavering faith and fortitude, have been given the grace to assist those who find themselves in the most dire and hopeless situations. We beseech you now to extend your compassionate hand to us as we pray for the resolution of seemingly insurmountable problems.

In the depths of our despair, when we feel overwhelmed by the magnitude of our difficulties and the futility of our efforts, we turn to you, St. Rita, as our refuge and our strength. We know that you, who once bore the wounds of Christ's Passion, understand our pain and can empathize with our struggles. We ask you to intercede on our behalf before the throne of God, that He may grant us the wisdom, strength, and perseverance necessary to confront and overcome the obstacles that lie before us.

We recognize that our trials are but fleeting moments in the grand tapestry of our lives, and that they serve to refine our faith and draw us closer to our Heavenly Father. Through your intercession, St. Rita, may we learn to trust more fully in His divine providence and submit ourselves to His will, even when we cannot discern the path that lies before us. Help us to cultivate a spirit of patience and endurance, that we may not falter or lose heart in the face of adversity.

In our darkest hours, when all hope seems lost and our hearts are heavy with sorrow, inspire us, O St. Rita, with your unwavering devotion to God and your steadfast commitment to prayer. Encourage us to persevere in our petitions and to approach our Heavenly Father with renewed confidence and trust, for we know that nothing is impossible for Him who created the heavens and the earth.

As we place our seemingly insurmountable problems into your loving hands, St. Rita, we ask that you guide and direct our efforts so that they may be in accordance with the will of God. Assist us in discerning the path to resolution, and grant us the courage and determination to follow it, no matter the challenges we may encounter. And as we strive to overcome our difficulties, may we never forget to give thanks and praise to our Heavenly Father, who alone can bring light out of darkness, and hope out of despair.

We ask this through Christ, our Lord, who lives and reigns with the Father and the Holy Spirit, forever and ever. Amen.

Prayers for Family and Forgiveness

St. Rita's incredible journey of patience, forgiveness, and love serves as a shining example for all those who seek to bring healing and harmony to their families and relationships. As a wife who persevered through a challenging marriage and forgave her husband's murderers, as well as a mother who prayed for her sons to abandon their quest for revenge, St. Rita embodies the virtues of forgiveness and reconciliation that are essential for fostering healthy and loving family dynamics.

In this chapter, we present five powerful prayers that call upon St. Rita's intercession for various aspects of family life and the need for forgiveness. By seeking her guidance and support, we can find solace and strength in her example and draw upon her wisdom as we navigate the complexities and challenges that often arise within our own families. Through St. Rita's intercession, may we be granted the grace to forgive, to heal, and to love unconditionally, just as she did throughout her life.

Prayer to St. Rita for Reconciliation and Forgiveness in Families

O gracious St. Rita, patroness of those in need of healing and reconciliation, I humbly approach you to seek your intercession for our families, who may be struggling with discord, resentment, and the pain of unforgiveness. In your boundless compassion, look upon us and guide us to the path of love, understanding, and unity.

Blessed St. Rita, through your life of sufferings and trials, you have shown us the transformative power of forgiveness, even in the most challenging circumstances. You, who bore the wounds of Christ, grant us the strength to bear our own wounds with patience, humility, and the willingness to forgive those who have hurt us. Teach us to let go of our grievances, and to embrace the healing balm of mercy that only our Lord can bestow.

Gentle St. Rita, help us to see the image of God in each member of our family, and to recognize the divine spark within them, no matter how dim it may seem at times. Inspire in us a spirit of humility and understanding, that we may seek to serve one another with love and selflessness, as Christ has served us. May our hearts be open to the grace of forgiveness, and may our homes become sanctuaries of peace, joy, and harmony.

Wise St. Rita, guide the hearts and minds of parents to lead their families with wisdom, love, and a spirit of sacrifice. May they be ever attentive to the needs of their children, nurturing their faith and fostering an atmosphere of forgiveness and reconciliation. Grant the gift of discernment to our children, that they may grow in their understanding of the importance of family unity and the power of forgiveness in their lives.

Most merciful St. Rita, through your intercession, may the Holy Spirit descend upon our families and fill us with His gifts of wisdom, understanding, and counsel. As we journey through this life, may we be ever mindful of the Lord's boundless mercy and be willing to extend that same mercy to our loved ones. In our moments of conflict and pain, may we always turn to you, St. Rita, for guidance, strength, and consolation.

In union with the Sacred Heart of Jesus and the Immaculate Heart of Mary, we ask this through Christ our Lord. Amen.

St. Rita's Prayer for the Protection of Children and Loved Ones

O glorious St. Rita, compassionate advocate of the troubled and afflicted, behold us, your humble servants, as we come before you, seeking your powerful intercession for the protection of our children and loved ones. We place our trust in your maternal care, confident in your unfailing assistance, and inspired by the shining example of your holy life.

Heavenly patroness of lost causes, you who persevered through trials and tribulations, and who found solace in the arms of our Lord, grant that our children and loved ones may be safeguarded from the perils and temptations of this world. May they be guided by the light of Christ, walk in His footsteps, and remain steadfast in faith, hope, and charity.

Through your tender mercy, St. Rita, let the love of Christ permeate the hearts of our children and loved ones, so they may grow in wisdom, strength, and understanding, and be nurtured in the bosom of the Holy Church. May the Holy Spirit inspire them to serve their neighbors, to act with compassion, and to always seek reconciliation and forgiveness.

In times of discord, O St. Rita, let your spirit of forgiveness and reconciliation descend upon our families, so that we may heal the wounds that divide us, and restore harmony and unity in our homes. As you forgave and prayed for those who caused you suffering, teach us to forgive those who have hurt us and to seek forgiveness from those we have wronged.

We beseech you, St. Rita, to intercede before the throne of our Heavenly Father, imploring His divine protection for our children and loved ones. May He bless them with His grace, shielding them from evil, and guiding them on the path to eternal salvation.

We humbly ask this through the merits of our Lord Jesus Christ, who suffered and died for our sake, and who now reigns with the Father and the Holy Spirit, one God, forever and ever. Amen.

Prayer for Unity and Harmony in the Family through St. Rita's Intercession

O Glorious St. Rita, patroness of impossible causes and source of hope for those in distress, we humbly implore your intercession on behalf of our family. As we face the challenges of daily life, we beseech you to grant us the grace of unity and harmony, that we may grow in love, understanding, and forgiveness. Through your heavenly intercession, may our family become a true reflection of the Holy Family, with Jesus Christ as our model and guide.

Almighty Father, who has bestowed upon us the gift of our family, we come before you with hearts filled with gratitude and humility. We acknowledge our imperfections and recognize the struggles that often arise among us. In these moments, we ask you to send forth your Holy Spirit, to enlighten our minds and soften our hearts, so that we may respond with charity and patience towards one another. May we learn to forgive as you have forgiven us, and to seek reconciliation when discord arises.

St. Rita, in your earthly life, you exemplified the virtues of humility, obedience, and patience. You bore the trials and tribulations of your family with unwavering faith and trust in the Lord. We implore you to intercede for our family, that we may likewise draw strength from the inexhaustible well of divine grace. Grant us the wisdom to discern the will of God in every situation, and the courage to follow His path, even when it seems difficult or impossible.

Through your powerful intercession, St. Rita, may our family become a beacon of light and hope for those around us. Inspire us to reach out with compassion and understanding to those who suffer, and to share the love and mercy of our Lord Jesus Christ with all whom we encounter. Teach us to value the uniqueness of each family member, and to celebrate the diverse gifts that each one brings to our family life.

We implore you, St. Rita, to obtain for us the grace of unity and harmony, that our family may become a living testament to the power of God's love. Through your intercession, may we be drawn ever closer to the heart of our Savior, Jesus Christ, who, with the Father and the Holy Spirit, lives and reigns, one God, forever and ever. Amen.

St. Rita's Prayer for Forgiveness and Healing in Marriage

O glorious St. Rita, patroness of those in need of healing and forgiveness within their marriages, we humbly come before you in our time of great need. With unwavering faith and trust, we ask you to intercede for our families, that the bonds of love, trust, and unity may be restored and strengthened.

In the name of the Father, the Son, and the Holy Spirit, we beseech you, St. Rita, to help us follow your shining example of forgiveness and compassion. May we learn from your unwavering commitment to love and harmony, even in the midst of great trials and tribulations. Teach us, O blessed saint, to persevere through the challenges we face in our marriages and to seek God's will in all things.

O gracious St. Rita, we implore your assistance in healing the wounds that have been inflicted upon our relationships. Through your powerful intercession, may the Holy Spirit guide us in recognizing the areas in our lives where we have fallen short and grant us the grace to seek forgiveness from our spouses, ourselves, and our Heavenly Father. Enable us to extend forgiveness to those who have wronged us, remembering the profound mercy and love that Christ has shown us on the Cross.

St. Rita, advocate of the brokenhearted, inspire us to find the courage and humility necessary to engage in honest and open dialogue with our spouses. Let the balm of God's love and mercy envelop our hearts, so that we may be instruments of healing and reconciliation for one another.

Pray that we may be patient with one another, bearing each other's burdens, and finding solace in the knowledge that Christ is with us in our struggles.

O holy St. Rita, we ask you to intercede on our behalf, that our marriages may be transformed through the divine grace of our Lord Jesus Christ. May our families be a reflection of the Holy Family, united in love, understanding, and forgiveness. By the power of the Holy Spirit, may our homes be sanctuaries of peace and joy, where the presence of God dwells in every heart.

Through your intercession, St. Rita, may the Lord grant us the strength to persevere in our marital commitment, to grow in virtue, and to deepen our love for one another, so that together, we may walk the path of salvation, hand in hand, until we reach our heavenly home. Amen.

Prayer for St. Rita's Guidance in Parenting and Family Life

O glorious Saint Rita, who by thy grace and divine guidance, art a loving intercessor for families and a beacon of forgiveness, we beseech thee to hear our humble prayer. As we navigate the challenges of parenting and family life, may we be ever mindful of God's presence in our homes and in our hearts, seeking His wisdom and assistance in nurturing the souls entrusted to our care.

In times of difficulty and confusion, we ask for thy intercession, O Saint Rita, that we may be granted the grace to foster a spirit of understanding, patience, and compassion within our families. May we be examples of Christ's boundless love and mercy to our children and spouses, and may we impart to them the virtues of faith, hope, and charity, which shall serve as a firm foundation in their journey towards the Heavenly Kingdom.

O admirable Saint Rita, thou who didst exemplify the essence of forgiveness and reconciliation, guide us in our quest to cultivate an atmosphere of harmony and unity within our families. Teach us to be ever attentive to the needs of our loved ones, and to extend forgiveness to those who have caused us pain or strife, so that we may imitate the boundless mercy of our Heavenly Father.

As we endeavor to raise our children in the light of faith, we beseech thee, O Saint Rita, to help us instill in them a deep reverence and love for the Holy Eucharist, devotion to the Blessed Virgin Mary, and commitment to the teachings of the Church. May we, as parents, always serve as models of virtue, humility, and prayer, inspiring in our children a lifelong commitment to God and His Church.

In times of trial and suffering, we turn to thee, O Saint Rita, ever confident in thy powerful intercession. May we find solace in the knowledge that God never abandons His children, and that His grace is sufficient to overcome all obstacles. We humbly implore thee to obtain for us the gift of perseverance, that we may remain steadfast in our faith and unwavering in our devotion, even amidst the storms of life.

O Saint Rita, patroness of difficult cases and impossible causes, we entrust our families to thy maternal care, confident that thou wilt obtain for us the graces necessary to guide our children and loved ones in the paths of holiness and righteousness. Amen.

Part IV: Supplementary Resources

Feast Day

The Feast Day of St. Rita of Cascia, celebrated on May 22nd each year, is a time to honor the extraordinary life and virtues of this remarkable saint. Known as the Patron Saint of impossible, lost, and forgotten causes, St. Rita's intercession is sought by people across the world, particularly those in need of healing, comfort, and hope. Her patronage extends to a wide array of groups and individuals, including wounded people, widows, victims of physical spouse abuse, sterile people, sick people, those struggling with parenthood, those in difficult marriages, and those suffering from bodily ills, loneliness, and infertility. In addition to these specific causes, St. Rita is also the patron saint of various cities and towns in Brazil, Italy, and the Philippines.

As the feast day approaches, devotees prepare to honor St. Rita through prayer, reflection, and acts of charity. Her life serves as a powerful reminder of the resilience of the human spirit and the transformative power of faith. The Feast Day celebrations often involve attending special Masses held in her honor, where the faithful gather to seek her intercession and to express gratitude for her powerful influence in their lives. In some regions, processions are held, with statues of St. Rita adorned with flowers being carried through the streets as an expression of reverence and devotion.

In her hometown of Cascia, Italy, the Feast Day of St. Rita is commemorated with much fervor and devotion. Pilgrims from around the world flock to the Basilica of St. Rita to attend the solemn liturgical celebrations, participate in prayers, and venerate her relics. The town comes alive with religious and cultural events, reflecting the deep connection between St. Rita and the community that cherishes her memory and legacy.

In Brazil, where St. Rita is venerated as the patron saint of various cities such as Viçosa, Ubaí, Sericita, Santa Rita do Sapucaí, Santa Rita do Itueto, Santa Rita do Ibitipoca, Santa Rita de Minas, Santa Rita de Jacutinga, Santa Rita de Caldas, Ritápolis, Presidente Olegário, and Nova Resende, among others, her feast day is marked by vibrant celebrations. Devotees organize novenas, special prayers, and Masses, expressing their gratitude for her intercession and seeking her continued guidance and protection.

Similarly, in the Philippines, St. Rita is revered as the patron saint of Igbaras, Iloilo, and Dalayap, where her feast day is observed with a unique blend of faith and cultural traditions. The faithful attend Masses and take part in processions, often accompanied by traditional music and dance, as a testament to their unwavering devotion to St. Rita and the hope and inspiration she represents.

The Feast Day of St. Rita transcends geographic boundaries, bringing together believers from diverse cultural backgrounds to celebrate her life, miracles, and enduring legacy. It is a day to remember the virtues that defined her existence - compassion, humility, patience, and unwavering faith - and to seek her intercession in our own lives. As we honor St. Rita on her feast day, let us strive to emulate her example, embodying her values in our daily lives and turning to her in our moments of need. Through her guidance and intercession, may we be inspired to face our challenges with courage and grace, confident in the knowledge that the Saint of Impossible Causes is watching over us, offering her support and comfort when we need it most.

Places of Worship

While we will focus on three major sites in this section, including the Basilica of St. Rita of Cascia, Santa Rita da Cascia in Campitelli, and Chiesa di Santa Rita da Cascia alle Vergini, it is important to note that there are many other churches and sanctuaries across the world that honor St. Rita. These places of worship serve as centers of devotion, prayer, and spiritual reflection, fostering a deeper understanding and appreciation for St. Rita's life and teachings.

Each place we will explore in this chapter uniquely connects to St. Rita, whether through the relics they house, their historical significance, or their artistic representations of her life. Through these sacred sites, devotees and pilgrims worldwide can experience a personal connection to St. Rita, drawing inspiration and strength from her unwavering faith and commitment to the Church. As we journey through these remarkable places of worship, may we deepen our understanding of St. Rita and her enduring legacy in the hearts and minds of the faithful.

The Basilica of St. Rita of Cascia

The Basilica of St. Rita of Cascia, located in Cascia, Italy, is a renowned place of worship dedicated to St. Rita. It was built in the early 20th century to accommodate the increasing number of pilgrims visiting the relics of St. Rita, which were housed in the old church that had become inadequate for such a large number of visitors. The construction of the new church was initiated by Mother Maria Teresa Fasce, the abbess of the nearby Monastery of St. Rita of Cascia, where St. Rita had lived for over 40 years.

"Sanctuary and Basilica of Santa Rita in Cascia"
by LigaDue/ CC BY-SA 4.0
https://creativecommons.org/licenses/by-sa/4.0/

The construction of the basilica faced financial challenges, and it was through the help of donations, including one from Pope Benedict XV, as well as funds raised through a newspaper called "Dalle Api alle Rose," that the construction was made possible. The design of the basilica was adjusted to fit the budget, and the final project was overseen by architects Giuseppe Calori and Giuseppe Martinenghi. The basilica was completed in 1947 and consecrated on May 18th of the same year. It was later elevated to the status of a minor basilica by Pope Pius XII on August 1, 1955.

The basilica's architecture is striking, with a white travertine facade and two spires, each topped with an iron cross. The main entrance portal bears an inscription in Latin, which translates to: "Hail Rita, vessel of love, sorrowful spouse of Christ, you, from the thorns of the Savior, are born beautiful like a rose." The columns supporting the entrance are adorned with bas-reliefs depicting scenes from St. Rita's life, created by Eros Pellini.

The interior of the basilica is shaped like a Greek cross and is divided into four apses, surrounded by a colonnade that supports an upper gallery. The walls feature stations of the Via Crucis, a pulpit, and a large neobyzantine-style fresco by Luigi Montanarini that covers the dome, lantern, sails, and four pillars. The fresco includes depictions of the Holy Spirit, St. Rita, St. Augustine, and other saints.

Within the basilica, there are several chapels and altars dedicated to various saints and events in St. Rita's life. The main altar is made of a crystal slab resting on gilded bronze grapevine branches and features a tabernacle designed by Giacomo Manzù. The Assumption Chapel features a painting of the Mother of Consolation with St. Augustine and St. Monica, while the St. Rita Chapel houses the glass reliquary containing St. Rita's body, which rests in a marble sarcophagus created by Eros Pellini in 1930.

The basilica also incorporates the older Church of St. Rita, which had housed her relics from 1577 to 1947. This older church is now used by the nuns from the nearby convent for their prayers. It contains several significant artworks, including paintings of St. Rita receiving the stigmata and the Madonna of Good Counsel, as well as a marble frame from 1629 that previously surrounded St. Rita's urn.

The Basilica of St. Rita of Cascia is a testament to St. Rita's life and legacy, serving as a place of worship and pilgrimage for the faithful from around the world. It stands as a symbol of devotion and inspiration, and a reminder of the power of faith and love.

Santa Rita da Cascia in Campitelli

"Le flanc et l'arrière de l'église."
by Palickap/CC BY-SA 4.0
https://creativecommons.org/licenses/by-sa/4.0/

Santa Rita da Cascia in Campitelli, also known as the Church of St. Rita of Cascia in Campitelli, is a deconsecrated church in Rome, Italy, situated in the rione Sant'Angelo, at the interChapter of Via Montanara and Via del Teatro Marcello. The church was built on top of the ancient San Biagio de Mercato, a church on the Insula Romana of Monte Capitolino, the remains of which were discovered during the dismantling of the church.

The church's history dates back to 1643 when architect Carlo Fontana constructed it over an earlier church built by the Bucabella family in the 11th century. This original church was located to the left of the base of the staircase of Santa Maria in Aracoeli and was dedicated to St. Blaise. Pope Alexander VI entrusted the church to the care of the "Confraternity of the Holy Crown of Thorns of Our Lord Jesus Christ." Devotion to St. Rita of Cascia was added to that of St. Blaise in 1900, the year of her canonization.

In 1928, due to several demolitions in the area to make

way for the Via del Mare (the modern Via del Teatro di Marcello), the church was dismantled piece by piece and preserved with the intention of being rebuilt at the same location. In 1904, the confraternity was forced to move to the former church of Santa Maria delle Vergini, which was reopened, re-consecrated, and re-dedicated to St. Rita of Cascia under the name of Santa Rita da Cascia alle Vergini.

However, the church was ultimately reconstructed in its current position in 1940, as commemorated by a plaque installed on site: "Questa chiesa già esistente alle falde del Campidoglio presso la scala di S. Maria in Aracoeli demolita nell'anno 1928, VI dell'era fascista, fu qui ricostruita a cura del Governatorato di Roma. 21 aprile 1940" ("This church, which already existed on the slopes of the Capitol Hill near the staircase of Santa Maria in Aracoeli, demolished in the year 1928, VI of the Fascist era, was rebuilt here by the Government of Rome. April 21, 1940").

Following the reconstruction, the confraternity, well-established in Santa Rita da Cascia alle Vergini, showed no further interest in the old church. Consequently, it was deconsecrated in 1990, and possession reverted to the city of Rome. The building, now known as the "Sala Santa Rita," is currently used for meetings, conferences, and musical concerts.

The church's facade is adorned with pilasters and stucco decorations. The interior follows a Greek cross plan with a convex rhomboidal design, similar to San Carlo alle Quattro Fontane. The deeper apse, compared to the side chapels, still houses the multicolored marble Baroque altar and the stained glass window depicting St. Rita of Cascia.

Above the transept stands the dome. The church's unique design and historical significance make it an important site for those interested in St. Rita's connection to places of worship.

Church of St. Rita of Cascia alla Vergini

In the heart of Rome, Italy, stands the beautiful Santa Rita da Cascia alle Vergini, a Roman Catholic church with a rich history and a strong connection to St. Rita of Cascia. Situated at the corner of Via delle Vergini and Via dell'Umiltà, this church offers a sanctuary for devotees of St. Rita who seek solace, guidance, and inspiration from her life and miracles.

Initially built in 1615 with the dedication 'Santa Maria delle Vergini,' the church was expanded and rebuilt between 1634 and 1636 to accommodate the needs of the neighboring Augustinian monks of the 'Collegio della Madonna del Rifugio.' The church's completion in 1660, with its facade attributed to Mattia de Rossi and the addition of a bell tower in 1689, marked a significant period in its history.

However, it was not until 1904, when the Chiesa di Santa Rita da Cascia in Campitelli was deconstructed to make way for the Vittorio Emanuele II Monument, that the church became closely associated with St. Rita of Cascia. The Confraternity of the Holy Crown of Thorns of Our Lord Savior Jesus Christ and of Saint Rita of Cascia relocated to the former church of Santa Maria delle Vergini. The church was then reopened, reconsecrated, and rededicated to Saint Rita of Cascia, serving as the national (regional) church of Umbria.

Designed in a Greek cross plan, the interior of Santa Rita da Cascia alle Vergini showcases Baroque decorations and the stunning dome fresco by Michelangelo Ricciolini, depicting the Glory of Paradise. The church also houses a gilded wooden organ, highlighting the intricacy of craftsmanship from that period. A chapel modeled after the grotto at Our Lady of Lourdes, dedicated in 1912, adds a unique feature that pays homage to the history and traditions of the Catholic faith.

As a place of worship dedicated to St. Rita of Cascia, the church plays a vital role in the spiritual lives of those who visit. St. Rita's presence within the church provides a beacon of hope and faith for those in need of her intercession. The church not only stands as a testament to the life and miracles of St. Rita but also offers a glimpse into the rich history and artistic heritage of the Catholic faith in Rome.

Main Events in the Life of St. Rita

- 1381: Margherita Lotti, later known as Rita, is born in Roccaporena, Italy.

- 1393: At age 12, Rita is married to Paolo Mancini, a rich and immoral man with many enemies.

- 1411: After 18 years of marriage, Rita converts her husband to a better person, renouncing the family feud known as La Vendetta.

- 1411-1412: Rita bears two sons, Giangiacomo Antonio and Paolo Maria, raising them in the Christian faith.

- 1419: Paolo Mancini is violently stabbed to death by Guido Chiqui, a member of the feuding family. Rita gives a public pardon to her husband's murderers at his funeral.

- 1420: Rita's sons, tutored by Bernardo Mancini, desire to avenge their father's murder. Rita prays for their removal from the cycle of vendettas, and they die of dysentery a year later.

- 1421: Rita seeks to enter the monastery of Saint Mary Magdalene in Cascia but is initially turned away due to the scandal of her husband's death and her non-virgin status.

- 1421-1422: With the help of her three patron saints, Rita reconciles her family with her husband's murderers, resolving the conflicts between the families.

- 1422: At age 36, Rita is allowed to enter the monastery of Saint Mary Magdalene. She is said to have been transported into the monastery by levitation at night by her patron saints.

- 1430s (approximate): Rita received a partial stigmata, a bleeding wound on her forehead, as a sign of her deep spiritual connection to Christ's suffering.

- 1440s (approximate): Rita becomes known for practicing mortification of the flesh and for the efficacy of her prayers, leading to various miracles being attributed to her intercession.

- 1457: Rita dies from tuberculosis on 22 May, after living by the Augustinian Rule in the monastery.

- 1607: Rita of Cascia is beatified by Pope Clement VIII, marking the beginning of her formal recognition as a saint in the Roman Catholic Church.

- 1900: Pope Leo XIII canonizes Rita on 24 May, bestowing the title of Patroness of Impossible Causes. Her feast day is celebrated on 22 May.

Afterword

Dear Reader,

I want to express my deepest appreciation and gratitude for joining me on this incredible exploration of the life of St. Rita of Cascia. As we ventured into her inspiring story, we delved into her unwavering faith, commitment to God, and the profound impact she made on the Catholic Church and the world at large. Thank you for your companionship on this enlightening journey into her life and the legacy she left behind.

Throughout this book, we have uncovered various aspects of St. Rita's remarkable character: her selflessness, her courage, her wisdom, her unconditional love for God and her fellow human beings, and her ability to overcome seemingly insurmountable obstacles. Through examining her extraordinary life, we have gained invaluable insights into her spiritual journey, relentless pursuit of peace, and influence on the Church's history.

As we retraced the steps of St. Rita's life, we encountered the events that forged her into the exceptional woman she became. We learned of her humble beginnings in Roccaporena, her marriage to Paolo Mancini at a young age, and her relentless determination to lead a life dedicated to holiness and service to others. We explored her unwavering commitment to her family, her endeavors to promote peace and forgiveness within her community, and the deep spiritual experiences that intensified her relationship with God.

St. Rita faced numerous trials and tribulations throughout her life, including an abusive marriage, the tragic deaths of her husband and sons, and the initial rejection from the monastery she longed to join. Despite these hardships, St. Rita's steadfast faith in God and her remarkable resilience enabled her to transform her suffering into a source of spiritual growth and strength. Her life is a powerful testament to the transformative power of faith, forgiveness, and love in the face of adversity.

One of St. Rita's most striking aspects is her ability to forgive and seek reconciliation, even in the most challenging circumstances. Her public pardon of her husband's murderers and her subsequent efforts to reconcile her family with his killers highlight her extraordinary capacity for forgiveness and demonstrate the healing power of mercy. St. Rita's example serves as a poignant reminder of the importance of forgiveness in our own lives and the potential for peace and unity that can be achieved through genuine reconciliation.

Moreover, despite numerous obstacles, St. Rita's unyielding devotion to God and her unwavering determination to follow her spiritual calling offers an inspiring example of perseverance and commitment to one's faith. Her life teaches us the importance of trusting in God's plan for us, even when faced with seemingly insurmountable challenges. St. Rita's story encourages us to remain steadfast in our faith and continually seek God's guidance and grace.

By writing this book, my aim was to bring St. Rita of Cascia's story to life and share her uplifting message with readers like you. I hope that by immersing ourselves in her world and learning from her example, we can draw strength and inspiration to persevere in our own faith journeys and serve as beacons of hope, love, and compassion.

As we conclude our journey together, I encourage you to reflect on the many lessons St. Rita has to teach us and to apply her wisdom and example to your life. By embracing the virtues of faith, forgiveness, and love, we can cultivate the resilience and strength necessary to overcome adversity and create a lasting impact on the world around us.

It has been an immense honor and privilege to delve into the life of this extraordinary saint, and I sincerely hope that you have found her story as captivating and inspiring as I have. As we embark on our own spiritual journeys, let us keep St. Rita's life and teachings in our hearts and minds, allowing her example of faith and devotion to guide us in becoming the best versions of ourselves for the glory of God. Amen.

"Let me, my Jesus, share in Thy suffering, at least one of Thy thorns."

—St. Rita of Cascia

Thank you!

We greatly value your feedback on this book and invite you to share your thoughts with us. As a growing independent publishing company, we are constantly striving to enhance the quality of our publications.

To make it easy for you to provide your insights, the QR code located to the right will directly lead you to the Amazon review page, where you can share your experience and offer any suggestions for improvement that you may have.

Related books

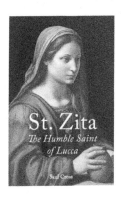

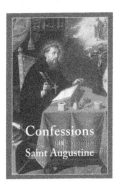

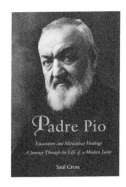

Scan the QR code below to browse our selection of related books and access exclusive supplemental materials:

Made in the USA
Monee, IL
27 August 2024

64595599R00075